Wabi-Sabi
at Work

All case studies and stories in this book have been altered to protect the privacy of our clients.
Any resemblance to a specific person or situation is unintentional.

ISBN: 1-4392-1653-3
ISBN-13: 9781439216538

Visit www.booksurge.com to order additional copies.

Wabi-Sabi
at Work

A Natural Path to Career Change

Whitney Greer & Gwen Woods

This book is dedicated to

all the clients, friends, family, and colleagues

who have become much more throughout the years

and have cheered us on in writing this book.

Table of Contents

Introduction

If you crave recognition for your natural strengths and passions by being authentic and true to yourself, then you're ready for Wabi-Sabi. Not to be confused with the green stuff you put on sushi that lights your mouth on fire, Wabi-Sabi is an ancient Japanese philosophy that values the natural, worn, and flawed. Think of a sea shell that you pick up on the beach and how different it is from all the others. No shell is *perfect*—each has distinction based on how the ocean shaped it over time. What shapes you? What distinguishes you? With a shift in perspective, you can learn to value all parts of who you are—including things you may have considered imperfections—and use these strengths, talents, and uniqueness to spark career opportunities.

This workbook will **transform your signature strengths and natural passions into career assets** by shifting perspective and teaching you to value who you are—the entire package—as well as discover what's getting in the way of gaining the recognition you deserve. Then we'll show you how to explore the environments where you can thrive.

Like its roots of impermanence, *Wabi-Sabi at Work* is a journey of inner and outer discovery that continues throughout an entire career, recognizing that the essence of a person may be the same, but situations, industries and businesses change, and we must evolve with them.

Over the course of more than a decade of workshops and one-on-one sessions, we've guided professionals and experienced first hand the joy and energy that comes from following a natural career path versus self-imposed milestones. Trying to be someone you're not and following a professional path you dislike saps energy and spins out or stalls a career. It happened to us when we accepted gigs where we donned the blue suit and turned on the PowerPoint, instead of rolling up our sleeves and problem solving through conversation. Our clients started seeing us as a training commodity— leaving us feeling like street walkers available to the highest bidder. What we were great at wasn't being valued or gaining us the distinction we wanted.

Our "aha" moment came during a gig in a locker room packed with rookie NHL hockey players who were learning to quote a party line. When one of us leaned back and found a jock strap stuck to her head, we knew we'd deviated from our natural path. By remembering to *walk our own walk* of being who we are—trainers devoted to teaching people to speak in genuine ways that connect with others versus throwing out bulleted messaging—we once again tapped into our passion and purpose.

If you stay buttoned up beneath a cloak that isn't who you are, you run the risk of being overlooked and unnoticed. For anyone from the newbie on the corporate scene, burned-out middle manager, or mom-or-pop-preneur who desires to find and apply his authentic differentiation in ways that clients, co-workers, friends, and family will applaud, we've created this guide.

Easy as A, B, C or A, C, B

We've designed this workbook with fun, guided exercises, and relatable stories about the universality of our foibles and the transformation others have experienced. Each chapter can be read in part during a lunch break or as a whole over a weekend.

In Chapters 1–3, you will discover the signature strengths that set you apart from the pack. A *Wabi-Sabi Pulse* takes inventory of what sparks you at work and where you're currently stuck. From that baseline, it's a tour de force of the Island of Conocos to separate instinct from habit, followed by a treasure hunt through your past accomplishments to find the underlying connections that can ignite new career opportunities.

Throughout Chapters 4–7, you look at how your actions, language, and image work for you or act as distraction. By eliminating the clutter of formulas that don't fit, or scripted conversations that leave you reaching for the antacid, you open the door to inspiration and motivation of a new kind. Once you identify the misperceptions and reasons for lack of recognition around key strengths, you will realign with your authentic self and showcase the talents and passions for which you want to be known.

Continuing in Chapters 7–10, your Wabi-Sabi journey turns toward the environments and settings where you shine best. Knowing that all career paths twist and turn and have highs and lows, Wabi-Sabi shifts perspective on how to flip, turn, or redirect perceived "flaws" or imperfections into strengths. By poking into new places of interest and passion while building genuine resource relationships, you'll discover how to navigate the changing landscape of a career so you are less bruised and more satisfied with where the course takes you.

Whether you dip a toe in to test the *Wabi-Sabi at Work* waters or jump in full force, approach this journey at a pace that works for you. If you already know your strengths, skip a few chapters and dive into language, image, or environment. The point is to use this workbook as a tool and apply what works for your current situation. If that means spending more time on one exercise and completely skipping another, we promise not to get our underwear in a twist.

Wabi-Sabi at Work ultimately represents a transition from formulaic thinking to a more genuine way of appearing. It replaces the script with improvisation, letting you live in the moment and like being there. Think of it as moving from generic to genuine as described below.

Generic	Genuine
A PowerPoint download	An exchange of ideas
"Crackberry" two-word email responses	Responsive, conversational sentences
Mandated visits with a coach or co-worker	Organic mentoring and wise counsel
Handing out twenty business cards	Resource connections and conversations
"Successory" motivational posters and dusty mission statements	Inspiration from real people
Three key messages	Stories with a point
Aiming for VP	Enjoying the professional journey
Being like everyone else	Being you

Wabi-Sabi isn't about letting it all hang out or letting go of goals. It's about valuing the journey and yourself, whether you are the veteran in your industry or leaping into a new field. It's about accepting who you are and how to let go of expectations, all while reconnecting with a more natural you.

Enjoy the journey.

— Whitney and Gwen

Chapter 1
I Yam What I Yam

When we tell clients they can be themselves and still be successful, they look at us like we just asked them to stand naked at a podium. After years of force fitting into an idealized mold and keeping their guard up, the words *just be yourself* sound like a pipe dream. These professionals are exhausted from trying to be what other people expect.

Breaking out of the mold and homing in on the authentic and natural strengths that transform careers isn't a magic pill that once swallowed instantly changes the situation. A successful and

Take a transformational pulse.

With a Wabi-Sabi Pulse to baseline your journey, you pinpoint how your strengths show up now and clarify your professional challenge. The foundation of Wabi-Sabi and those who have walked the path before you, like Jon Stewart (The Daily Show) and Katherine Graham (The Washington Post), provide clear examples of how a career is transformed when you use your strengths and talents in the right context.

satisfying career involves knowing which opportunities to go after and which to throw out the window, building strong resources long before you need them and finding your way through the clouds of perceptions swirling around you. It's easy during a career journey to beat yourself up for not being the right kind of "leader" who can motivate thousands with three sentences while managing budgets of zillions, or you may even wonder why after all the years of steady progress you haven't made it to the level you thought you would and aptly deserve at this point.

Read the leading management and career self-help books, and you'll have a series of "aha" moments that potentially leave you ready to strive harder and faster but a few months later are lost and forgotten. This workbook isn't about solving your career ills in a nanosecond or following a series of 1, 2, 3 steps to professional stardom. *Wabi-Sabi at Work* is about looking at your career through a different lens—one that lets you draw on the strengths that differentiate you from others and one that values the experiences and perspective you accrue on the journey. It's time to begin your Wabi-Sabi journey.

Our approach is based on Wabi-Sabi, a philosophy honoring the authentic and natural—even the imperfect. In fact, what looks flawed, like a bubble in a piece of hand-blown glass or a nick in a piece of furniture, is what sets one item apart from the other. It's what you do with your "imperfection" that makes the bigger story.

The Unintentional Wabi-Sabi-ist

According to Jon Stewart, of Comedy Central's *The Daily Show* fame, he couldn't make much sense of his wildly careening career path until he learned to embrace his irrepressible humor. From his early days, Stewart's unbridled sense of the absurd caused him trouble. Whether it was during a high school play, where he pretended to pee on a tree, or as a Woolworth's shelf stocker fired by his own brother for diving from a bean bag into a group of aquariums and causing $10,000 in damages, Stewart comments that his raw sense of humor acted as a career-limiting trait. It was only when he found the right environment that he transformed into a powerhouse comedian distinguished for his off-the-cuff topical humor.

Jon Stewart is what we call an unintentional Wabi-Sabi-ist. He could have continued to fight or hide his distinctive brand of humor (although even he admits it was impossible for him to stay on the straight and narrow for long) but instead, he chose to "own it." Like Popeye, he learned to say, "I yam what I yam and that's all what I yam."

It doesn't matter that Jon Stewart, like most unintentional Wabi-Sabi-ists, probably never heard of this sixteenth-century Asian philosophy embracing imperfection and impermanence. We'd never heard of it during the many years we trained high-profile executives and spokespeople how to tap into their natural strengths to better tackle challenging situations. Yet, we were living and applying the philosophy in our own lives and practice all along.

The Heart of Wabi-Sabi

Wabi stems from the root *wa*, which refers to harmony, peace, tranquility, and balance. Today, it means simple, unmaterialistic, humble by choice, and in tune with nature. Someone who is perfectly herself and never craves to be anything else would be described as Wabi.

Sabi means "the bloom of time." The meaning of the word has changed from its ancient definition "to be desolate" to taking pleasure in things that are old and faded. In our practice, the word applies to valuing what you've accomplished—the whole story of your experience, not just the milestone events. In Stewart's case, what could have been a series of ego-bruising events turned into fodder for his comedic career.

At work, someone who is Wabi-Sabi is willing to drop the façade of perfection—the formulaic Über-leader—and own his or her individual imperfections as part of the uniqueness and strength he or she brings to others and to critical situations. Often the context of these so-called flaws is what gives them power. A flaw in one environment becomes strength in another. The chatterbox keeping us from checking off items on our to-do list may actually be the person most likely to motivate a team during crisis. When given a proposal to write, the dreamer can be our best visionary.

Social Butterfly or National Asset?

The late Katherine Graham, who became publisher and head of *The Washington Post* following her husband's untimely death, possessed signature relational strengths that served her well as a hostess for Washington's Who's Who, but she was initially dismissed as frivolous in the newspaper world. Despite skeptics who saw her only as a party hostess and criticized her for having no business experience, she set out to win the loyalty and trust of hardboiled journalists.

How did she manage it? The relational strengths she demonstrated as a social networker became the backbone of her ability to build ties. In the reporting game, where knowing who's got your back can make the difference between cracking a story or missing a scoop, Graham's writers trusted her enough to take on controversial issues like Watergate and Vietnam, winning the paper many prestigious awards.

Graham reached the pinnacle of publishing success even though she didn't fit the conventional leadership mold or arrive armed with an MBA in her holster. In fact, her relational gift, initially considered a liability, proved to be her career-defining characteristic.

You can't be recognized for your greatest talents, whether that's nurturing teams, networking or problem solving creatively, by waiting for other people to identify them or by taking a test. You live these talents daily throughout your life, often forgetting to value and apply them at work.

Throughout the development journey we offer in this book, you assess what's great about you, in a way no performance reviews can. You explore Wabi-Sabi and integrate it into the workplace in order to change a situation where you are stuck and promote your career. There is no A, B, C formula to follow. Instead, we guide you on a series of discovery exercises, offer perspective on people we believe embody *Wabi-Sabi at Work*, and share stories from the many clients who have transitioned into new careers, new roles, and new levels of satisfaction through "aha" moments translated into action.

We invite you to tackle your largest career challenges by changing your perspective and being in the moment so opportunity finds you. When you approach a career in this way, you flip the circumstances where your strengths aren't valued and rekindle your potential by being in the right settings.

Flip It

One of our favorite clients, a 25-year sales veteran, learned the lesson of unappreciated strengths the hard way. After being hired for his talent of ferreting out a client's underlying challenge beyond the immediate request and determining a resource match, he found that his strength was no longer valued.

Jeff had earned his reputation over time and developed a loyal base of high-profile clients who saw him as a trusted source. He landed large accounts other companies salivated over, but the bigger they were, the longer they took to close. Unfortunately, his new supervisor, a push-product-and-make-the-numbers guy, didn't value Jeff's approach. He prescribed a sales formula for turning every client conversation into an immediate sale.

Threatened with the loss of his job, Jeff complied, choking down the bitter pill. Clients resented Jeff's *new* approach. They didn't believe he had their best interests in mind. Ultimately his sales suffered, and his confidence slipped. Fast forward a few months and Jeff, once a top performer, found himself in last place.

What went wrong? In the wrong place, with people who didn't value his ability, Jeff acted in an inauthentic way, shutting down his signature strengths and stalling out his career. We're glad to report, however, that Jeff eventually recovered.

To determine where you may be missing the mark because you haven't discovered your signature strengths or aren't putting them to use, we invite you to take a Wabi-Sabi Pulse.

Discovery Exercise: A Wabi-Sabi Pulse

1. What strengths and traits do you want to be known and recognized for professionally?

    Having a hard time figuring out what you bring to the table? That's okay because we'll work with you to uncover your differentiation in the next chapter.

2. What are you getting recognition for right now?

3. What projects and roles spark your energy?

    Think about the projects and environments where you suddenly lose track of time because you're so engaged.

4. What is motivating you to transform your career?

    - *I'm out of work or in a work setting that requires immediate change.*
    - *I need to explore new career opportunities in my current workplace or in other companies.*
    - *I'm new to the job and want to start off on the right foot.*
    - *I'm re-entering after a break from the workforce.*
    - *I want or need to move into a completely new field of work.*
    - *Other:*

Whether you're a budding entrepreneur, a benchwarmer on the management team, a career changer, or someone re-entering the workforce, being fully yourself brings power and energy. Once you stop fixing perceived flaws from the past or covering what you think is wrong, you're free to seize opportunities as they arise. *Wabi-Sabi at Work* creates opportunity to showcase your true colors at the right time, in context, and in your best environment.

Aha! to Action: A Wabi-Sabi Reflection

A glance in the mirror says a lot. Take this week to assess when you feel most comfortable, accomplished, and in command. This builds on the Wabi-Sabi Pulse exercise described above and targets the areas where you are sparked and engaged.

Aha!

I'm most comfortable and powerful when I…

Example: "…get to share an insight with somebody or problem solve." Or, "…have input on decision-making."

The Action

Keep this information with you as you move forward to uncover more of the great things about you and your abilities.

Wabi-Sabi Grace Notes

- ✓ *Wabi-Sabi values who you are—the entire package.*
- ✓ *Imperfections when seen in another light can become defining strengths.*
- ✓ *Your strengths and experience differentiate you from other people in a way that can gain you the recognition you want.*
- ✓ *Wabi-Sabi should not be confused with wasabi, the green paste on your sushi.*

Chapter 2
A Trip to the Island

When we ask people to list their strengths, we invariably hear a litany of test results and performance feedback instead of what's real to them. They say things like:

"I'm direct."

"I get a job done."

"I problem solve."

While these answers may be true, they are limited. Accept them as the whole story, and you can miss the panoramic view of your true strengths.

Wabi-Sabi at Work allows you to identify the multitude of strengths you possess outside other people's definitions by viewing yourself through

Test your strength.

From the Island of Conocos to the comfortable language of your tribe, you will uncover insights into your basic instincts at work. The Wabi-Sabi tea ceremony illustrates valuing your strengths in ways that set you apart instead of falling into habitual roles like the "note taker" or "office therapist." You'll add to the strength list by inviting people to tour your rebuilt island and translating the results into "how" you do your work.

multiple lenses—in expansive moments, during a regular routine, and under pressure. Sometimes your greatest strengths surface outside of your job, as you throw a party and discover an ability to manage large scale projects or support a sick relative better than anyone else because of your intuitive nursing skills. Sometimes your strengths lie beneath the surface, only bubbling up during pressure situations that push you beyond your comfort zone. Take, for example, when you're the only cool head able to recover data after a computer virus wrecks the hard drive or when you instantly find just the right candidate for a headhunting friend because of your unparalleled networking ability.

Basic Instincts

What are your instinctive talents when the heat is on? Jumping in and taking action? Analyzing? Organizing? A trip to the Island of Conocos uncovers which basic instincts you can add to your *Wabi-Sabi at Work* strengths.

Discovery Exercise: The Heat is On

While on a long overdue vacation to the Island of Conocos, a devastating hurricane hits, wiping out the village and outside communications. The inhabitants select you as their new chief and look to you for guidance. Your first instincts are to:

a) Gather the tribe together, find out the impact of the hurricane and assuage fears; make an inspiring speech that encourages people to take action.
b) Send a team to assess the damage and collect data for repairs and reconstruction; consider population growth estimates, management costs, and return on investment.

c) Develop a phased rollout system that outlines improvements complete with assigned task teams and a timeline.

d) Brainstorm possibilities for the island including a new connector bridge, high speed and wireless web access, parks and recreation areas.

In this exercise there is no right or wrong answer, just information. Don't over-think your answer. Go with your first inclination. (If picking two options feels right, go with it.) Depending on which option you chose above and the matching letter below, you are someone who:

a) Benefits from strong relational ties, often putting the welfare of others before your own;

b) Is comfortable with analytical thinking, assessing a situation before taking action;

c) Loves process and an established plan; or

d) Peers into the future, visualizing what can be.

Okay, maybe you aren't actually the chief of an island struck by a hurricane—at least, not this week. But you've probably encountered some stressful circumstances that forced you to make quick decisions. Think back over the last week or two at work. Was there a highly charged situation in which you were a key player? What was your gut response? Write it here.

Does this instinctual behavior correlate with any of the above a-to-d options? If not, you may have discovered a new strength. Hold onto that thought.

Tribal Language

Acting on instinct may not be the way that you uncover your basic strength. Some people identify their strengths by observing where they are most comfortable—during meetings, facing new projects and managing teams—and with whom they are most comfortable. In other words, finding the people who speak their language.

To discover which island tribe you resonate with most—the relationals, the operationals, the visionaries, or the analytics—we offer a language guide. Find the phrases you'd be most likely to use in a day-to-day conversation.

Dialect of the Operational:
Checklist, prioritize, schedule, timeline, phases, task force

Commonly Used Phrases and Questions:
How do we plan to get this done?
What is the timing for this project?
What are our priorities?
Who's involved and what are the responsibilities?

Dialect of the Visionary:

Envision, create, imagine, innovate, design, cutting-edge, trend-setting, Eureka!

Commonly Used Phrases and Questions:

And then we can…

What about if we…

I've been thinking…

OOOO, OOOO…

How can we expand that idea?

Dialect of the Analytic:

Examine, evaluate, consider, question, outcome, forecast, ramifications

Commonly Used Phrases and Questions:

Does this make sense for the organization?

Is it logical?

How will this impact us down the line?

What's the return on investment?

If you look at this from both sides…

Let me play Devil's Advocate…

Dialect of the Relational:

Collaborate, connection, teamwork, relationship, motivation, rally

Commonly Used Phrases and Language:

How will this affect morale?

Have we had a meeting on this yet?

Can we meet face-to-face on this?

What about [insert name]? Have we considered his feelings?

Let's collaborate.

Which language patterns did you fall into? Remember, you're not one-dimensional, so you may have experienced crossover between two tribes. Consider these responses as part of your strength mix (operational with a high degree of analytical or innovator and a twist of relational).

Once you've identified the basic instincts that drive you in both life and work, you have valuable information about the essence of your *Wabi-Sabi at Work* self. However, proceed with caution. While gut impulses can serve you well at getting you out of tight situations, without thought as to how and where to activate instincts, they can become habits others take for granted and don't always appreciate. Howard learned to transform his habitual instincts into valued strengths when he changed where and how his innate desire to organize kicked in.

Force of Nature or Force of Habit

Howard worked with a creative marketing group that frequently spiraled out of control and lost focus when brainstorming. As someone who loved to stay on point, he volunteered to capture ideas and format them in executive summaries. After a few months of meticulous editing and bulleting, Howard made a disheartening discovery when a chance reference to a past report met with blank stares. No one was reading his hours of painstaking work.

Instead of launching his laptop against the wall in frustration, he took a step back from the situation. When once again the group started to wander off topic—this time over moving a proposed launch date—Howard didn't just take notes to be sent out later. This time, he offered to step up to the whiteboard and organize information in real time. With the pros and cons clearly before them, the group quickly made a decision. Taking his talent real-time and in a more visible place like the whiteboard transformed him from Howard the Note-Taker to Howard the Strategic Facilitator.

Think about your own habits. Are you always the banker on family game night? Do you relate to Lucy in the *Peanuts* comic strip, unconsciously mounting a "The Therapist Is In" sign on your office wall and letting people come in with their problems at all hours? Do co-workers shake you like the Magic 8-Ball™ when they need direction? Where have your basic instincts become habits instead of assets?

Time for Tea

Bringing value back to a habit doesn't require a big production. Legend has it a Wabi-Sabi tea master brought value back to what had become a showy display of finery and pomp when he poured tea in simple, clay cups and held the ceremony in a rustic location. By focusing on the experience of the tea first and foremost, and by removing the elaborate set-up and circumstance, he gave significance back to something that had become rote.

Paying fresh attention to your instincts can also give meaning to them in a different way. Setting a specific time when you can truly listen to an officemate's problem transforms you from an emotional ER open to everyone to an appointment-only private practice. Writing a note stating why you believe an article is relevant to the reader, instead of automatically hitting the group list, shows more analytic, big picture thinking rather than highlighting your clipping services. How and where you let basic instincts serve you can change your reception and recognition.

Instincts aren't the only strengths taken for granted when they become habit or routine. People often forget that what differentiates them from someone else isn't what they do, but how they do it. Two people can hold the same title and engage in similar work but complete their roles using very different strengths. One web designer may start with copy, another with examples of sites the client loves. Both can experience equal success. Wabi-Sabi allows for individuality. There is no right or wrong, no "perfect" way in which to reach a goal—just the way that works best for you.

A Tale of Two Realtors

Candice, a successful realtor and passionate photographer, rose to the challenge when faced with buyers short on time and long on restrictions. A young couple, new to the area, was on deadline to finish construction on a coffee shop and find a home before their lease ran out. Instead of competing with hammering construction workers, Candice put her artist's vision to work. She created a photographic pictorial of her favorite homes and neighborhoods (even finding art pieces to complement the space) and compiled them in a customized laptop house tour. She met her deadline, sealing the deal on a property before the buyers ever set foot in it.

Tracy, also a successful realtor, came at a similar challenge from another angle. When two high-profile executives on constant travel told her to find them a home, she drew on her skill of customizing the shopping experience. During the first face-to-face interview, she walked them through a detailed thirty-minute questionnaire covering everything from aesthetic preferences to garage layout. With answers in hand, Tracy pre-shopped available homes, narrowing the choices down to five that met their criteria. They spent one morning touring before making a decision the same day.

Candice's creativity and Tracy's customization strengths both resulted in client satisfaction. If each realtor had stopped to worry about doing the job the "right" way, both would have missed the sale. To zero in on the *how* of what you do—your unique imprint—we head back to the island, but this time inviting some friends along.

Discovery Exercise: An Island Excursion

The island is now rebuilt to your specifications, and you're ready to share your handiwork. Describe the experience you would create for visitors including where you would take them and why (the solar power plant, schools, parks, etc.); what they would see, touch, smell and eat along the way.

Wendy's Example:

When people arrive, they are greeted by soft music playing from speakers disguised as coconuts in the trees. I offer a refreshing fresh fruit drink in a bamboo eco-friendly cup and invite them to relax in cushy chairs on an open-air, shaded pavilion on the beach. They order from a menu of tapas-style island foods.

We tour the village on a moveable solar-powered sidewalk. Visitors can choose where they go—craft studios, homes, a school, a hospital, a communal dining hall, or the physical plant. Guests will stay in small groups with a host family to experience the island life first hand.

When Wendy reviewed her island experience, certain descriptions jumped out at her. She highlighted them and translated what they said about her and how they related to her work as a customer service representative.

Wendy's Translations:

On the Island:
- *Soft music playing, refreshing drink, cushy chairs = putting others at ease; keeping the atmosphere relaxed.*

On the Job:
- *During customer calls she uses a soothing, conversational tone to calm customers — especially those with a problem.*

On the Island:
- *Speakers designed as coconuts; a beach view = attention to aesthetics.*

On the Job:
- *When listening in meetings, she mutes her phone so other people on the line won't have to hear competitive phone noise in the background. If she sends an email, she spell checks and makes sure it is well worded.*

On the Island:
- *A tapas menu and choice on where to tour = customizing an experience.*

On the Job:
- *Whenever possible, she offers callers an A or B selection (e.g., I can have you hold while I investigate or call you back within a half hour) to solve an issue so they feel she is catering to them.*

Where did you focus your attention: on the experience, the demonstration of innovation, or the next phase of development? Highlight the descriptions that jump out the most for you. What do your answers say about you?

Some possible translations to consider:

Sharing food = creating a sensory or nurturing experience

Interest in infrastructure = passion for how things work

Interaction with villagers = connection with others

Festival/celebration = sparked by big event moments

Technology = interest in innovation or process efficiency

Your Translation:

When you stop taking your own instincts and inborn talents for granted, you can allow them to surface in new ways that give them value. Before you rush to highlight these strengths, let them simmer for a while. Pay attention and honor them without trying to change or squelch them. If you fall into an old pattern, don't beat yourself up, write it down. There's still more to your unique strength story.

Aha! to Action: Out of Habit

The idea of valuing what you have in a new way is so critical in this chapter, we want you to take specific action around the strengths that have become habit or you've taken for granted.

Aha!

This week write down any habits you fall into or a time when you devalue a talent by taking it for granted. (You agree to track the budget even though it's not part of your job, you say you'll rewrite a friend's resume, you offer to take the old computer equipment to the recycling center, etc.)

1.

2.

3.

4.

Action

List changes you can make to your timing, or the environment, to allow your instinctual and natural strengths to be valued more fully.

1.

2.

3.

4.

Wabi-Sabi Grace Notes

✓ *Instincts can be part of your unique strengths.*

✓ *When instincts become habit, they lose value.*

✓ *"How" you do what you do differentiates you from others.*

✓ *You can kick habits and turn them to strengths by changing the time, place, or way you put them into play.*

Chapter 3
Buried Treasure

Remember scavenger hunts? You would run from house to house and yard to yard to find the elusive four-leaf clover or the empty Coca-Cola™ bottle. These items didn't seem significant. Yet, whoever gathered the most items became the winner, and as a result the stray 1962 penny became a sought-after treasure.

In this chapter, we challenge you to hunt through your history for the seemingly unimportant experiences that could be your hidden treasure. If reliving your big hair days or wild ways makes you shudder, there's a good reason to rummage

Unearth your forgotten treasures.

Connect to underlying strengths collecting dust in your professional or personal attic. Instead of ditching your old baggage, rummage through and see what's been lost and forgotten. Turning the mundane into treasure is an important part of Wabi-Sabi at Work.

through your past. You only have to watch *Antiques Roadshow* on PBS to see how an ordinary vase gains value when its history is revealed. Maybe you didn't survive the Civil War or live in a famous person's attic, but in *Wabi-Sabi at Work* your experience as a volunteer, caregiver, or editor of your school newspaper may be more than passing interests. They may be your collection of valuable differentiators.

Stashed Away

When we met Nelta, a veteran in television ad sales, she didn't have a clue about her own cache of hidden talent. She had moved through a one-track media career at a fast clip, but stalled at director level. A single-minded focus led Nelta to value only one thing: the ability to leap levels in a corporate setting.

"I can't believe I'm almost forty and haven't made VP yet," she confessed.

When we asked, "What have you been doing for the past ten years aside from your day-to-day work?" her face went blank. But then her cell phone interrupted us, and, excusing herself, she was suddenly transformed. She became completely absorbed in the conversation—and spoke in flawless Italian!

It turned out Nelta spoke three languages, had lived overseas in two countries, and loved hosting get-togethers for international visitors. While she fully acknowledged these feats, she didn't understand how fearlessly stepping into new cultures or bringing people together was relevant to her current career goals.

By reviewing her accomplishments outside of work, and linking those experiences to her signature strengths, Nelta rediscovered that she was a strong, never-say-never individual who thrived on tackling new situations. Her international perspective and ability to step into other cultures were career assets she could trade as professional currency.

Later, chatting with a collegue about overseas travel, Nelta inadvertently recognized a route into some new career opportunities involving international client work and country-to-country advertising projects that went beyond her vice presidential destination.

With similar exploration of your interests and experiences, you can reclaim signature strengths you've stashed away and open up new possibilities for your career.

My Life in a Scrapbook

Recently Whitney found out that her mother had created a scrapbook of every letter, poem, and story she had written from the age of seven on. Reading through these, she remembered what an eloquent young writer she had been. In the photos of her at age twenty backpacking on the Appalachian Trail, she recognized the nature-loving explorer who eventually moved cross-country twice. Old articles on the Ya Ya Business Club she started told the tale of someone who created resources where none existed.

Even if no one has played historian for you with a personalized scrapbook, you can create a mental version of your own.

Discovery Exercise: Your Wabi-Sabi Life Book

Flip through old photo albums, yearbooks, or thank-you cards from the bottom of your junk drawer. What do these images and notes say about your abilities and what sparked you in the past?

Here's what to look for:

Candid photos from life events (weddings, holidays, reunions, preschool, etc.)
Note the settings and people you are with when you appear most energized.

Yearbooks
Look beyond your hair and read the comments from your classmates to see what they recognized about you.

Past resumes, cover letters, and interview communications (including jobs you didn't get)
What were you shooting for and how did people respond?

College application and recommendations
What qualities have others captured about you?

Notes and emails
What were you recognized for?

Awards and certificates from grade school on (even if it's a third grade contest you won for designing an advertisement)
Find the natural talent you had way back when.

Personal letters, cards, and communications sent for birthdays, holidays, or just because
How are others describing what you mean to them?

Team and club involvement
What were your interests and pursuits?

Imagine some of these moments and victories captured in a real scrapbook. Feel free to do this by memory, or get out the glue stick and old photos and make this a book you can hold. If computer graphics are your preference, a digital version may be a more fun option. What strikes you most about your past and present?

What's in the Attic

We're often told to "let go of the baggage" and focus on the future. In a classic *Wabi-Sabi at Work* turnaround, we suggest you rummage through your attic and see the great stuff you've been saving. There's value in the musty, dusty, and forgotten as Cesar found out in a surprising way.

Cesar's career path took a circuitous route leading him from a double major in urban planning and behavioral sciences to work in high-tech, where jobs were more plentiful. What started out as a temporary post in the marketing department to pay the bills eventually led to a full-time job. Cesar let go of his academic training and repositioned himself as a marketing expert. As his career advanced, he left his academic accomplishments by the conversational roadside, thinking of them as irrelevant during interviews.

Much to Cesar's surprise, his background became significant again during his first assignment at a hot marketing agency when he had to pitch Northern California's largest homebuilder. The builders were blown away by his design and structural knowledge, and as a result of speaking their language, he won the account. When it came to anticipating and managing clients, his behavioral sciences background became a distinguishing ace-in-the-hole.

Just because you can't use it today doesn't mean your experience won't prove handy tomorrow. Play this matching game by drawing a line between the background you think correctly matches the professional path our client eventually took.

Buried Treasure	**Career Link**
1. Educational background in journalism and creative writing.	A. Love of innovation and technology opened the doors to a whole new line of cutting edge products when this professional moved into the family pool business.
2. IT work at a technology start-up during dot-com bubble.	B. After a long career in sports marketing, this entrepreneur rekindled her passion by donning her writer's cap, blogging and creating web content.
3. Fundraising and volunteer management for annual AIDS walk.	C. At a rally speech, this person stepped up to motivate and direct a large group and was invited to take a leadership position on the board of a selective nonprofit foundation.
4. Summer internship spent traveling and touring South America to learn Spanish.	D. In a competitive job market, this person rose to the top by connecting international retail distribution centers together with language translation skills.

The view around the career bend may elude us until we get there, but there's usually a logical transition. Here's how past experiences led to present value for the people described above: 1–B; 2–A; 3–C, 4–D. Maybe you didn't realize that an event would have future significance in your career. Yet the clues exist. Your past reveals the signature strengths you've demonstrated over and over, possibly without realizing it. Some of your *Wabi-Sabi at Work* treasures may present themselves in gritty and less spectacular ways than you would expect. However, if you pull these underlying strengths out and dust them off, you'll see a theme emerge.

A Thread of Gold

Jesse Ventura, wrestler turned Minnesota governor, is a man with a colorful past whose career turns at first glance seem surprising. Closer examination shows a common thread—his core strengths—running between his uncommon life and work.

As a Navy Seal who served in Vietnam, Ventura put his life on the line repeatedly, and his risk tolerance can be seen throughout his career. During his smack-down wrestling heyday, he spoke loudly and often. Leaving the tight shorts behind to enter political life as Governor of Minnesota, he tackled topics other politicians often avoided, like religion and prostitution. Later, hosting a syndicated television and radio show, he aired his often controversial perspectives. When he did a stint as a visiting professor at Harvard, his lectures explored the parallels between professional wrestling and politics.

What connected his dots? Ventura's outspoken, no-holds-barred approach—a style that allowed him to assert his beliefs while under fire. He refused to fall into the spin trap by hiding behind popular opinion and pleasing an audience—a route that would have diluted and devalued his *Wabi-Sabi at Work* strengths while submerging his authenticity.

Do any of your responses in this chapter support or add to what you discovered about your signature strengths? Did you dust off a favorite pastime and find value for it today? To bring your full *Wabi-Sabi at Work* package into view, the Aha! to Action section will be a Fully Monty (that's the naked truth) one-stop wrap-up. With a full picture of your natural talents and well-honed strengths, you're ready to transform your career choices.

Aha! to Action: The Full Monty Recap

No, we're not pressing you to join a nudist colony or forcing you in front of the mirror in your birthday suit. Instead, we're urging you to reveal your *Wabi-Sabi at Work* strengths in their full glory.

Aha!

Write down the **signature strengths** you unveiled during previous chapters and exercises.

Your basic instincts during your trip to the Island of Conocos in Chapter 2.

Your Wabi-Sabi Hidden Treasure findings from this chapter.

Action

Now that you have your *Wabi-Sabi at Work* signature strengths front and center, it's time to make some choices about which deserve more exposure.

List your discovered signature strengths, placing those you embrace most first.

1. _____

2. _____

3. _____

4. _____

Remember when we asked you what you wanted to be recognized for in the Wabi-Sabi Pulse in Chapter 1? Do any of these descriptions fit the bill? Which are new? Which are the ones that you didn't or don't know how to value? It's time to break out of the behavior mold and build the right perceptions around these abilities and strengths.

Wabi-Sabi Grace Notes

✓ *Relics from the past add up to valuable career assets today.*

✓ *Bringing past experience out of the closet and giving it a place of recognition is a Wabi-Sabi way of valuing your natural talent.*

✓ *The activities and passions you follow throughout your life are stitched together by the thread of in-born natural strength.*

Chapter 4
Formula Busters

The essential style needed to become an Über-leader seems to vary like spring fashion, swinging wildly and frequently. Media and leadership gurus hold up icons who embrace the classic model of the General Electric CEO, exuding efficiency, or the newer model of the hipster, rumpled and renegade. Both types are described as having "unending stamina" and being "intensely competitive." (If you modeled yourself after Carly Fiorina, the hard-charging "Master Strategist" CEO ousted from Hewlett-Packard, you became quickly outdated. The "it" leader who followed, Meg Whitman, previous CEO of eBay, built her leadership brand around consensus building and motivation. Her style became the de facto standard for female leadership.)

Break out of molds and models that don't fit.

Becoming Wabi-Sabi at Work *means being comfortable in your own skin. Instead of falling into a formula trap, transform the prescribed step-by-step formulas into authentic behaviors.*

So what's the current style for success? And how are you supposed to remake yourself in the image of the icon *du jour* so you can innovate, take risks, mobilize teams, and read industry shifts all at the same time?

Fortunately, the answer is that **you don't have to conform to be successful**. In fact, if you choose to adhere religiously to the behaviors, languages, and images of your icons, you risk losing what's best about *you*.

Who Wants to Be Margaret Thatcher?

"I'll never be a Margaret Thatcher," said Mary, an 18-year non-profit veteran. She picked this quintessential conservative diplomat as her role model after receiving a verbal slap for barreling over a co-worker with her blunt style. From direct and to the point, Mary quickly morphed her sharp perspective into comments like "I hope you're okay with us doing it this way…" While she didn't ruffle as many feathers, she lost her impact.

Mary admired Margaret Thatcher, because she embodied convention and the ability to build relational bridges—traits Mary lacked. But this template was not a good fit. While her instincts to develop and balance her style were sensible, it was as though she were forcing herself into an ill-fitting suit. Instead of finding the right time and place to act naturally as her straight-shooting self, she became a passive player.

We encouraged Mary to show her true colors and urged her, when she was in a tricky spot, to use Margaret Thatcher's attitudes as models, not replacements for her behavior. During emotionally charged meetings, she took a more diplomatic approach acknowledging all the players' input and ideas before weighing in quickly with her own solution.

Transforming a Formula to a Fit

Acting natural generally produces better results. It keeps you from reaching for the Pepto-Bismol® bottle after behaving in ways that go against your grain. *Wabi-Sabi at Work* is not about formulas and striving to be someone you aren't. To be *Wabi-Sabi at Work* means accepting yourself and being comfortable in your own skin.

What often gets in the way of following our instincts when it comes to behavior, words, and image, is that we're programmed at work to act and speak in ways that keep us homogenous—in other words, we adopt formulas. Formulas that bind us are anything from an unrealistic role model to the "it's always been done this way" department motto.

Formulas show up everywhere; from the thirty-second elevator pitch to overused buzzwords. Awareness is the first step toward making choices about what inspires and what locks you into alien behaviors. See if you recognize any of the standard practices below and give yourself kudos if you've already broken the mold.

Cut the Cable on the Elevator Pitch

When one person asks another, "What do you do?" the person answering often pushes the mental "play" button and launches into pitch mode. He or she assumes the position, standing straighter and locking eyes. The thirty-second elevator spiel is in rerun mode with bored viewers wishing they could fast-forward past the commercial.

TIP: *Contrast this scenario with a more genuine approach. Instead of turning on a one-way infomercial download, why not build a conversation? Don't tick off job description bullets. Share a recent project or moment that jazzed you. When you're sparked, others will be interested.*

The PowerPoint Crutch

If we had a dime for every time someone comes into a workshop with a 40-slide PowerPoint multimedia show for a 10-minute presentation, we'd be sipping Mai Tais on the beach right now. Ask why they need a laptop loaded with slides to make three key points, and most people confess that while they hate the format, it's what's expected.

When a senior vice president asked us to help her prepare her acceptance speech for an industry award for creativity, we didn't realize it would involve a design team. In walked two graphic artists, one publicist, her assistant, and a multi-media specialist. Ironically, she was considered the creative one. As the PowerPoint slides started to pile up with data and market research, we had to speak up. Herding out her posse, we asked her to tell her own story.

She reached a transformational moment when she kicked the PowerPoint habit and presented her amazing professional journey with only one graphic slide she designed herself and used as a backdrop. When she received a standing ovation, it was for more than an outstanding presentation. The crowd approval was also for someone who had dared to buck the conventional approach and showed up as her true *Wabi-Sabi at Work* self.

TIP: *Images speak louder than words and aren't as hard on the eyes as a laundry list of bullets. Create your notes first, not your slides. Think about an image or graphic that would enhance the point you're making. Need inspiration? Download any speech from a product launch given by Steve Jobs of Apple.*

Buzzwords That Won't Die

We know the B.S. quotient of a company by the length of its buzzword list. Despite having lost all meaning, terms like *ubiquitous, leverage,* and *value proposition* are still flashed around like the latest cell phones.

During a meeting where the word *systemic* puzzled a group of executives, one savvy manager looked it up only to find out it was being used incorrectly. The inside joke cracked this team up every time another manager repeated the mistake. We say, rely on your brains, not buzz.

TIP: *Go with quick description, detail, an individual perspective, and conversational language over marketing-speak. When people can see it, smell it, and taste it, your description is working and the connection is made. If you wouldn't use the language in conversation over coffee, strike it from your vocabulary.*

Swimming in a Sea of Clones

Because we travel a lot, we've seen a range of fashion formulas. In New York it's about wearing black; in L.A. the shoes matter and don't even get us started on convention khakis. These uniforms are scary reminders of high school, where wearing what everyone else had on seemed important. Imagine the satisfaction of wearing a memorable red jacket among a sea of forgettable blue and black suits.

TIP: *Does your current business wardrobe reflect anything about your individual qualities? (A screenwriter we know promoting a teleplay with a feline theme wore her favorite cat pin to networking events as a conversation starter.) If you must coordinate with a group, make an outfit your own with a particular cut or color. Many hair salons mandate black clothing for employees, but each stylist interprets this in a unique way.*

Discovery Exercise: From Icon to Inspiring

Are you finding inspiration from the icons and formulas swirling on your sonar? Are you using them to spark new ways of showing who you are?

Read through the magazines and books on your desk or nightstand that profile successful people or offer advice. Think about the last speaker you heard and his or her recommendations.

How many different formulas for success can you identify?

1. _____

2. _____

3. _____

4. _____

Pick two of the examples you found. What message is being communicated?

1. _____

2. _____

What inspires you about this message?

1. _____

2. _____

What part of this message seems unrealistic or impossible for you to achieve? Write down what should be discarded into the recycling bin.

1. _____

2. _____

Here are our two examples:

<u>Gwen:</u>

I read a great article on Richard Branson and how he finds investors. In one case, he was looking for a smaller (just under $1 million) investment from his longtime banking partner to upgrade equipment on some of his airplanes. The partner refused him, and he had a moment of hesitation around his decision making. Branson reviewed his plan again and decided that if his bank didn't believe in his ideas enough, he would find someone else who did. He found another investor, who lent him several hundred million dollars, and he bought a new fleet of airplanes.

Inspiration: Always be willing to pursue new options and partners.

Toss into the recycling bin: The idea that I will ever be as big of a risk taker as Richard Branson. There's no way, no how, and to try to become like him would just make me feel inadequate. Instead, I'll take the message of looking in all sorts of places for resources and see if they apply to my business situations.

Whitney:
Recently I read *Floor Samples*, the biography of Julia Cameron, author of my favorite creative guide, *The Artist's Way*. During some of her most productive years writing screenplays and books, she struggled with relationships and alcoholism. She speaks of these problems unflinchingly.

Inspiration: Being a writer is not a series of goals, but a lifelong journey of the heart. You don't have to produce a dozen books and screenplays to call yourself a writer. When you're writing, you're a writer.

Toss into the recycling bin: Cameron's journey is one of frequent creative suffering and isolation—two concepts I don't believe have to be part of the creative's life equation.

Finding inspiration from what you read can have far more impact on your career than following every piece of advice like a recipe (where one missed move means a flattened soufflé). Looking at role models and formulas for ideas that interest you lets you expand on the places where you'll find a career-defining spark. Soon you'll see your local wine merchant or fellow train commuter in a whole different light. We received a great tip about selling a business from someone sitting nearby on a plane who had just sold his. Enjoy the freedom to poke around anywhere and everywhere for ideas and motivation while busting out of formulas that would otherwise dictate your next steps for you.

Aha! to Action: An Original

Break-out moves seem to happen overnight, but sometimes they're an accumulation of years of thought and effort. Boost your original thinking with some outside power and then start the change.

Aha!

Finding inspiration in all the right and new places means that I will explore:

✓ New reading material that I don't normally pick up.

✓ An environment that stimulates my mind in a new way.

✓ Bouncing an idea off someone whose perspective is different from mine.

✓ Other:

Action

List the first formula you will lose. How might you replace it with a more natural action?

Wabi-Sabi Grace Notes

✓ *Stepping out of the strictures of icons and Über-leaders allows your individuality to surface.*

✓ *Once you've broken out of formulaic thinking and behaviors, there's opportunity for natural expression of words, actions and images to support your strengths.*

✓ *Role models, as sources of inspiration versus prescriptions for success, can open your eyes to new or expanded ways of showing up in the world.*

Chapter 5
Caught in the Act

Paul Potts, the first winner of *Britain's Got Talent,* sent chills down the spine of many listeners with his intensely passionate, operatic voice. During interviews, he was bashful and not the typical slicked-up, over-polished "star." Yet when the public voted, they connected so strongly with his authentic and heart-felt performances that he won acclaim and a record label. Moving from the facade of perfection to letting your strengths and passions speak for you is *Wabi-Sabi at Work.*

Align your actions with your natural strengths.

Learn to pay attention and then authentically gain recognition for being yourself. When people perceive you as the Speedy Brander or the Gregarious Sportscaster, your actions may not be consistently demonstrating your Wabi-Sabi at Work *strengths.*

When you're consistently *caught in the act* of being your best self, people offer you new projects and more responsibility. You don't have to sell yourself. In this chapter we look at how your actions and everyday behaviors shape the perceptions of others about your signature strengths. You'll break bad habits, deal with misperceptions, and take initiative where it supports your strengths the most.

Better Mousetrap Man

One of the best examples we know of someone whose actions align with his natural strengths is a software consultant who built his reputation on a passion for building the better mousetrap. An innovative thinker, he could improve on almost any process—whether it involved brewing beer, working out, or billing clients.

At a luncheon where he was updating his division head about his activities, the topic turned to the company's sales incentive difficulties. Although the issue was outside his charter, our innovator proposed a solution that the executive found intriguing. Fast forward a month, when the division head contacted our client from across the country to solicit his ideas and ultimately hire him to handle another company challenge.

By acting authentically, as his *Wabi-Sabi at Work* self, our innovator gained visibility and a reputation for problem solving that naturally led to opportunity. He didn't have to perform or make a big production to be recognized for his strengths. He simply behaved authentically and consistently.

The Speedy Brander

Instead of showing talent in a natural way, many people contort themselves into a pretzel, taking on any and every project to gain recognition. This was the mistake made by the Speedy Brander, a talented woman who became known for the wrong accomplishments. She arrived on our doorstep with a scatter-shot resume in hand, concerned that what people wanted from her wasn't what she did best.

A quick analysis of her work history told the story of someone who let circumstance dictate her behavior. While she wanted to work with a company that had a long-term vision and understood the power of building brand loyalty over time, her money had run low and she needed a gig. She decided to consult until she found her fit. After talking to us, she identified a pattern.

"The accomplishments I talk about, and the work I continue to accept, reflect someone who can build a brand in 90 days, not someone creative or big-picture oriented. No wonder these cash-crunched start-ups keep coming to me. They know I'll kill myself to meet their unrealistic goals," she said.

We counseled our client to define which short-term opportunities would support the *Wabi-Sabi at Work* strengths she wanted to emphasize. Instead of leading with another hoop-jumping, miracle-working case study, we suggested she emphasize her planning, strategy, and creative thinking for the client. Eventually she networked her way to a well-funded start up that gave her the breathing room she needed to pilot a breakthrough campaign and seal the reputation she wanted.

Sometimes out of circumstantial need, we make hasty decisions that derail long-term goals. Other times, through a lack of awareness about our actions and their impact, we distract others from seeing our real abilities.

How can you tell if your actions are tipping the perceptual scales in the wrong direction? There are two sides to every story and to every action.

How you show who you are may be a matter of taking too much of one action, like editing every piece of paper that comes across your screen or desk, pegging you as the editorial nit-picker. Or always asking "why" and poking holes when people need quick action. In this exercise, we stack up the daily actions favoring your *Wabi-Sabi at Work* strengths against those unbalancing the perceptions you want.

Discovery Exercise: Tipping the Perceptual Scales

Fill one side of the scale with the places and people that enable you to successfully show your true colors through the course of a day.

<u>Side A</u>

Who are you with and what are you doing?

Example: I regularly conduct a staff meeting where I ask each person about their projects and facilitate quick solutions from the group.

Fill the other side of the scale with places and people where you continually have to explain yourself, or you're unsure of what they think about your ability.

<u>Side B</u>

Who are you with and what are you doing?

Example: Every time I run into my supervisor, I hurry to download everything I'm working on, because she doesn't read anything I send her. She probably believes I'm always in a rush, and I feel like I'm wasting her time.

Review what you wrote. Can you identify any habitual behaviors like taking on assignments you don't want because saying no might create conflict? Are you avoiding participating in a meeting because you don't want to say something wrong? Is there a certain person or group that brings out an alter-ego in you? Once you've identified your habits, you can begin modifying how you handle a situation.

How you react to people and situations gives you a big picture overview of the messages your behaviors may be sending. Don't overlook those physical habits—the nail biting kind—as they send messages as well. A few of the negative perception-setting actions we've seen include constant fidgeting, whirlwind entries into meetings, agenda-cramming two hours of information into a thirty-second elevator ride, and curt hallway greetings, or worse, none at all. These may be distracting from your signature strengths.

The Great Sportscaster

Frank, a gregarious industry analyst, had a habit of popping into offices of his colleagues to share his enthusiasm for his favorite football or baseball team. He failed to notice how their eyes darted to their computers as he went on about the latest stats. Where he thought he was making a connection, his supervisor saw someone who didn't know when to shut up—a fact he shared during our initial pre-coaching audit. The supervisor drew the conclusion that Frank couldn't be trusted to deal well with clients, which was a career buster as Frank's next promotion depended on managing critical negotiations.

During a coaching session, Frank commented that his wife often complained about his annoying habit of sharing information at inopportune times. It was clear he'd been getting the right feedback for a long time but didn't know the implications.

To get Frank back on track so others could see his *Wabi-Sabi at Work* self, we encouraged him to become a master observer and note what happened during his interactions. When did people engage and ask questions? When did they say "uh-huh" and give him the brush-off?

Once Frank figured out what was happening, he learned to limit his small talk to dead times during meetings (like when early birds wait for the laggards to arrive). He also exchanged small talk for discussions about hot industry topics. A month passed, and Frank reported that people appeared more willing to chat with him and sought him out for his opinion on industry events. Frank's reputation as an industry analyst improved enormously. To his supervisor he'd become someone clients could respect. In less than six months, Frank received a much-desired promotion.

Nicknames, Jokes, and Nagging—Oh My!

Nicknames and comments said in jest are also big clues to how your actions are being perceived. You may hear these in your professional or personal life. For example:

- You walk into a meeting and someone says, "I see we're running on Paul time today."
  – A gentle poke at a more serious tendency toward tardiness.
- You're introduced to a peer as "Tangent."
  – Indicating a tendency to go off point during conversations.
- Your spouse talks about your propensity to turn into a "hurricane" when the going gets tough.
  – Points to a frazzled state of mind during stress moments.
- Other team members gripe when you start playing devil's advocate.
  – Signals a naysayer who rains on others' parades.

Note the nicknames or comments people repeat about you in jest. Keep in mind that these nicknames may not be negative. However, they may indicate a discrepancy between what you want to be recognized for and where you're getting attention.

Queen of Events

Rena, a mid-level promotions manager with a strong performance record, was the workhorse of her team and an innovative launch expert. Though she was capable of rubbing elbows with the most powerful executives from the accounts she managed, she met regularly only with the gatekeepers.

In a bid for better visibility, she volunteered to put together the holiday party, knowing that many of the attendees would be high level. She planned for months to wow clients with a different kind of event—a Cajun party complete with Zydeco band and dance instructor. The festivities were in full swing when the agency owner waved Rena over. He had beside him the owner of the company whose account she managed, but whom she had never met.

Rena had to clutch her cocktail to keep it from crashing to the ground, along with her dignity, when the agency owner introduced her as "Rita, our Event Queen." While the owner waxed on about the amazing event, he never once mentioned her outstanding work as the creative promotional expert behind several of the client's key launches. Clearly Rena's hard work and actions hadn't translated into the right kind of attention.

Realizing she'd been tagged as the team's "doer," and not as a master strategist or creative force, Rena went into realignment mode by:

- Asking for, and being granted, the chance to present an update on her team's latest product launch success in a senior management meeting. (She gained her supervisor's buy-in by recommending he present the larger vision first and then have her on hand to add in details and answer questions on the rationale behind the creative decisions she'd made.)

Later a senior partner asked her to join his project for some fresh thinking.

- Circulating a few choice articles on viral marketing with notes on how the agency could apply ideas in a new way to current accounts.

    Her ideas were discussed among senior management as a gain for the entire agency.

- Booking herself (with agency approval) as a panel speaker for an association conference highlighting her latest case study.

    Word spread that Rena was making a name for the agency as an innovative competitor out in the bigger world.

- Encouraging her team to create a game plan that included regular check-in points instead of her managing each step.

    This was necessary to gain time for the other actions and served as a step toward empowering her team.

Discovery Exercise: An Action Adjustment

The following exercise is intended to help you fix misperceptions. Below we name the strengths and actions that detract. For each insight into a negative situation, think of an action adjustment to correct the problem.

1. **Strengths: analytic, strategic-thinker**

   Aha! *"Sitting at the back of the room during meetings is causing others to see me as disengaged."*

   I'd like to be seen as involved. Proposed action adjustment:

2. **Strengths: creative, problem-solver, collaborator**

   Aha! *"When I pop into my supervisor's office to discuss an idea and ask her opinion, she thinks I have a problem I can't solve."*

   I want her to see me as solutions focused. Proposed action adjustment:

3. **Strengths: organized, efficient, keeps others on track**

   Aha! *"When I come into a meeting with a full agenda instead of a conversation, people tell me I'm steamrolling them."*

   I want to be recognized for tapping into other people's expertise. Proposed action adjustment:

Some possible action adjustments you may or may not have considered include:

Adjustment #1: Get in early, use the time to discuss a topic in your area of expertise and help someone else. Ask questions during the meeting or volunteer to organize information at the whiteboard.

Adjustment #2: There's an expectation for people to self-manage. To demonstrate problem solving and collaboration, don't dip into a supervisor's well over and over. Instead, bounce ideas off of other people. When presenting an idea, make sure it's about something important and offer solutions before soliciting input.

Adjustment #3: Less is more. Don't cram too much into a tight time-slot. Determine which items need real face-time and which can be handled at a different moment. Balance this routine with conversation as people arrive.

To Be Taken in Small Doses

When dealing with misperceptions, the knee-jerk reaction is to attempt a personality overhaul. Al Gore did just that during the 2000 presidential election campaign. Criticized for his stiff delivery at the podium and lack of warmth, he did an about face on the campaign trail, donning a flannel shirt, growing a beard, and speaking with a drawl from his native state of Tennessee. Predictably, people responded by focusing more on his image overhaul than the fact that he was capable of being a regular guy.

On the other hand, Al Gore's conversion into the prophet of global warming aligned his behavior with his beliefs. He was transformed into a man with a mission who also happened to win a Nobel Peace Prize and an Oscar®.

The moral of the story is that you want people to realize you've made changes after they think about it, not because the change is the first thing they notice about you.

Aha! to Action: All Hands on Deck

A single action is like a finger held up for attention. Notice how much more attention you can get with all five fingers waving.

Aha!

Choose five ways you're currently getting noticed.

    1.

    2.

    3.

    4.

    5.

Action

Pick five actions you will swap, drop, or add to gain the kind of attention you want.

1.

2.

3.

4.

5.

Wabi-Sabi Grace Notes

✓ *When you act naturally, you create opportunity to show your best self to others.*

✓ *Forced actions appear false and are hard to maintain.*

✓ *Small, incremental action adjustments will bring your* Wabi-Sabi at Work *self into focus more fully.*

✓ *Creating perceptions about yourself that groove with your strengths takes awareness; too much or too little and your perceptions will be out of balance.*

Chapter 6
Express Yourself

Turn on the five o'clock news in any city across the country and you'll watch local newscasters who seem as interchangeable as LEGO® parts. These generic "talking heads" share the same voice inflection, accents, pausing, pacing and language choices. To break into the big time status of someone like Katie Couric, known for her warm tenacity, or Anderson Cooper, willing to wade into uncomfortable situations on behalf of people in need, budding reporters must demonstrate great journalistic skills and communicate in ways that let people understand their approach. In other words, unveil their personality. These reporters write their own pieces and deliver them in the unique way only they can.

Find natural language that reflects your best self and creates connection.

Wabi-Sabi at Work is about true connections and leaving indelible impressions. When you worry less about coming across flawlessly in all situations, you open the door to a verbal exchange rather than a download of information.

This chapter encourages you to spark connections through natural and authentic expression, not as a picture-perfect talking head. We'll encourage you to infuse a dose of your personality into emails and reports, instead of writing every missive like a heavily-edited term paper. When you **worry less about flawless communications and more about building a connection**—whether with one person or hundreds—you can begin a *Wabi-Sabi at Work* conversation.

How do we characterize a true *Wabi-Sabi at Work* conversation?

Is	Is Not
Sharing a story	Boring bullets
Description	Overused buzzwords
Insights and perspectives	Over-quoted party lines
Extemporaneous	PowerPoint perfect
A flexible agenda	A script
Audience needs	Your wants
Colloquialisms	Webster's words
Accented	Newscaster diction
Asking and listening	An elevator pitch
An exchange	A download

The idea here is to keep it real, not to deliver what you think other people expect to hear at the expense of losing your originality.

Ripping Out the Page

Our client Alex learned the value of a *Wabi-Sabi at Work* approach to communications after her textbook answers to a questionnaire earned her a rejection from a prestigious association board instead of a hoped for in-person interview.

Alex couldn't understand why the review committee had turned down someone with her stellar credentials and solid experience. Based on what we knew about Alex this puzzled us, too.

We asked to see the application she'd submitted and immediately ferreted out the culprit. Alex's answers reflected nothing of her true experience and made her sound like every other applicant. When asked to describe her management style, she wrote:

I am a hands-on manager leading a group of twenty-five people. We work on a variety of projects ranging from interactive web content to music contracts. My budget is more than $25 million.

The rest of her answers followed the same generic template. Not one response revealed a woman talented at cherry-picking teams and motivating them to accomplish huge, industry trend-setting projects.

To help Alex find and express her story, we pulled on our investigative reporting caps and drilled down into her work life. We interviewed her on how she overcame challenges and mobilized teams at work. Every time she made a statement, we asked her to give us a real-world example. What resulted caught our ear, as well as the attention of the application committee. The second time she applied, she wrote:

I build in-house dream teams from around the globe to create high-profile launches within a $25 million operating budget. Through an internal website, I facilitate weekly web meetings and online project *downloads to keep my team moving at entrepreneurial speed. Our most recent Zap Phone launch generated an eighty percent return on investment.*

Her second application succeeded in intriguing the board enough to have them invite her to tell them more. During her face-to-face interview, she threw out the pre-packaged self-marketing script and shared relevant, first-hand stories, as well as asked thoughtful questions. We're pleased to report that Alex was unanimously approved to join the board.

To help you tell your story in a way that pops, we invite you to borrow a page from Alex and storytellers everywhere.

Discovery Exercise: What's Your Story?

Even when you aren't caught in the act of highlighting your strengths through behaviors that can be seen, you can speak volumes about yourself through a great story. In this exercise, we encourage you dig beyond the ten-bullet laundry list response to answer the question, "What do you do?"

Describe something you do, or a recent project you enjoyed.
Example: I'm a mental health advocate for low income families who've been denied coverage.

Add detail and description. Use your senses, what do you see, touch and hear?
Example: I pull together our team, go through the toughest cases to problem-solve, and find a good solution.

Personalize your response by adding a specific example.
Example: I had to find a way for one homeless man to get his medication dispensed at a shelter so the healthcare company would cover his mental illness. There is always an answer if you dig around long enough. I love finding the solutions.

Read back over what you wrote. Did you remember to mention the challenges you overcame? The outcome? Can you add quantitative information, so that you offer someone a highlights tour, not a dissertation? Underline the segments that pop to your eye or ear, and the ones that say the most about your *Wabi-Sabi at Work* strengths. Prioritize what's most important to get across first and last.

Now you've got the idea of how to build a story that says something about you in a way that engages the listener.

A Language Overhaul

In order for people to hear your amazing story, you'll want to eliminate any verbal distractions. These include speech patterns or word choices that undermine your *Wabi-Sabi at Work* strengths.

Watch out for ambiguous language. Like the CEO who during a merger announcement to the press, consistently repeated the phrases, "We're hoping to and trying to." We pointed out that it's difficult for someone to invest in a company where the CEO sounds as if he's unsure he can meet his goals.

When describing your actions, be specific. Some Sloppy Joe language to mop up includes:

- **I've worked on …**
  Swap with: I orchestrated, pioneered, expedited, sparked, solidified, designed, and facilitated.
  Active language places you in the action. If you're using passive language, you're positioning yourself as the worker bee not a driver.

- **Hoping or trying to…**
  Swap with: I am, I'm in process of…, We're exploring…

- **It's kind of, sort of like…**
  Swap with: It is!
  Ambiguous language sends messages of insecurity. If you're not on the case, who is?

Beware of lazy speech habits. "You know," it's "like" they "kinda" cause high school flashbacks. Unless you're comparing two items, we classify the ever-present word *like* as a four-letter word. You only have to listen to someone who inserts it between every other word to smell the gym shoes.

Steer clear of up-speak. You might as well wear a "Hi, I'm insecure!" label on your jacket if it sounds as though you're ending every sentence with a question mark. Nervous speakers tend to introduce themselves by inflecting up, causing listeners to wonder if they know their own name. To assess if you've contracted the up-speak virus, play your voicemail message.

The antidote for any of these problems includes a dose of mindfulness followed by a willingness to replace your question with a statement. To retrain your ear and voice, we recommend a conversational do-over instead of wishing you had said it differently after you hang up or leave the room. Preface your correction with "What I meant to say is…." Caution, you only get two of these per conversation or you may start to sound like someone who doesn't know what they want to say. Pick the worst habit you're correcting first. After a while, the right word choices and inflection become just as habitual as the old.

When a Little Means a Lot

Too much of a good thing can also kill a communication. Here are the top conversation door-closers we continue to see in person and in print:

- Issuing directions without a relational touch may earn you the nickname Sarge.

Tip: Remember a greeting and smile before launching. Review emails before hitting the send button and warm up the intro and close.

- Too many hallway conversations can peg the overly chatty as "time- wasters".

Tip: If what you need to say is longer than three minutes, schedule a meeting with the other person.

- Collaborative types who constantly ask, "What do you think…" send the message they can't find solutions on their own.

Tip: Wait until you really need feedback and don't continue to drill the same resources for answers.

- Poking holes in everyone else's plans to play devil's advocate and sounding like the group naysayer.

Tip: Replace "this won't work because…" with a solutions focus on how "this could work even better is if we…"

We're not here to make you paranoid, just mindful. Cleaning your verbal house clears space for better conversations. Now that you've looked at losing distractions and strengthened your story-telling skills, it's time to engage. By engage we mean talking with, not at someone else.

Witness a job interview from the hiring side of the table, or attend a networking event where you ask someone, "What do you do?" and you've probably experienced the talking *at* phenomenon. That's where the person launches into a ten-minute introductory pitch, or a play-by-play of their last decade. **Speaking for more than a few minutes before asking a question sucks the oxygen from the room**.

Building a Better Conversational House

We speak from experience. A contractor we encountered caused us to gasp for air from his long-winded pitch.

Experienced and well-referenced, the contractor in question, Matt, took his own walk of fame when he should have noticed the little people around him. We mean that literally. As the homeowner struggled to corral her two nap-deprived children, he laid out a pile of news clippings and flipped open a large marketing binder. Instead of growing impressed as he listed his many accomplishments, the homeowner grew irritated. Desperate to move on, she asked if they could get to her proposal.

What went wrong? Matt's dog-and-pony show did nothing to address the woman's specific and immediate concerns—her home and the children in it. To the homeowner, Matt appeared unconcerned about the immediate situation. The homeowner wondered how concerned he'd be about her big building challenges. In his preoccupation with his own agenda, Matt forgot to place his audience's needs and wants first.

Holding Open the Verbal Door

Wabi-Sabi at Work communications place the person listening or reading ahead of your own agenda. In the tea ceremony you pour for the other person first. **In conversation, you give someone your full attention by recognizing their interests and circumstances**.

For the harried mother who didn't have a lot of time, the contractor should have noticed she had her hands full and responded by condensing his introduction way, way down. Instead of competing for her attention, he should have asked her a couple of questions to zero in on the information she wanted most. So what if he didn't cover everything on his agenda? At least she would have spoken to him again. Before leaving, Matt could have solidified the relationship by sorting through his pile of articles and finding one with relevant tips to leave behind or send later as a touch back. When you give someone your full consideration, you're holding the door and they can step into a conversation with ease.

Discovery Exercise: In the Know

To open the door to great conversations, tune in to the people around you. How can you give them greater consideration? Start by sharpening your powers of observation.

Pick someone you plan to speak with soon.

What type of information perks up their ears?
Ex: The homeowner would have responded to a quick overview of her project followed by the contractor's ideas.

How does this person like their information served up?
Ex: That twenty-five-page in-depth binder the contractor so proudly deposited on her table? Save the paper. When time is of the essence, busy people want you to cut to the chase. The one-page executive summary followed by a source for more in-depth information is a failsafe option.

Rules of Engagement

If nothing comes to mind about your audience, you may need to dig deeper. We've been hearing recently from HR recruiters that the practice of researching a company is becoming a lost art. Even in our own company, we interviewed more than forty people before finding two who checked us out further than our website.

Reading articles or the news section of a company's site lets you know the other person's perspective. For example, a pending reorganization tops the worry list. If your conversation deals with anything past the reorganization, you won't make it beyond the first sentence unless you start by acknowledging the elephant in the room.

Start the conversation with what's happening now and link those events to your subject. One option is to say, "While there are organizational changes occurring, _____ is relevant right now because…" If you can't make the case for relevance, hold for later.

Before launching into conversation, **stop and get a pulse** for what's happening with the other person. We know of one ambitious and deserving professional who went in to ask for a promotion right as her boss received a call from a family member with bad news. The communication went south when he kept asking her to repeat her case. If she'd observed his concerned face and asked, "Is this a good time?" she could have avoided what became a difficult exchange. When you know what's happening in someone else's world, you can adapt your conversation and timing to build a stronger connection.

If you can't uncover someone's preferences for information, ask. Do they like email or prefer face time? Do they need frequent contact or regularly scheduled check-ins with a place to go on their own for more information? Your mission is to find what works best for them.

Find Common Ground

Sometimes it's difficult to know where to begin, which is why so many people seem to dread networking events. At weddings, the rules of engagement with strangers are clearly defined. People find natural common ground by asking "Whose side are you with? The bride or the groom?"

At a professional networking meetings the question, "How are you associated with the event?" serves the same purpose.

Some great openers to adapt include, "What interested you about this panel?" or "What did you think of the speaker?"

Go for the *how, why,* and *what did you think* questions to avoid the yes/no response. Becoming an interrogator puts the other person on the spot and closes the conversation down. After two questions, it's your turn to share. Try these and the suggestions below to develop your personal process for making conversational magic.

Discovery Exercise: Making Conversational Magic

The alchemy of authentic *Wabi-Sabi at Work* conversation comes from showing excellence and establishing a connection while being you. To create conversational magic, follow the exercise below.

- Imagine you're speaking with the person from the "In the Know" discovery exercise above. What would you like to have happen in this conversation? What is your intention?

  Ex: I want to explore the industry they're in to find new business or career opportunities.

- Prepare questions you can ask during a conversation to discover more about the other person and establish common ground.

  Ex: How did you get involved in ____?

  What type of information are you tracking?

- Think of an insight, observation, opinion, or quick story relevant to the listener you can share.

  Ex: Your recent announcements on _____ made me think of _____.

  Currently, I'm ____ [insert your story].

  From what I've read, it appears your company is____ [insert your analysis here].

  Based on street buzz, it sounds as if _____ [insert your insight].

  That's similar to a situation I experienced when _____ [insert your story].

• During your conversation, you can create the next opportunity to engage.
  Ex: Perhaps we could continue this conversation…
  I have some additional information I'd like to share…
  If this is a topic you enjoy, I can…

Read aloud what you've written. Does what you wrote accurately reflect your *Wabi-Sabi at Work* strengths and sound authentic? Revise anything that sounds too formal or out of character.

When you test these out in the world, know that they may not have the exact outcome you expect. Connections, like chemistry, vary depending on circumstances and situation. Not getting the exchange you wanted? Don't force a connection—if it doesn't happen, find a graceful way to move on.

Beyond networking events, you can build connections in your everyday world and explore new territory with old sources. At a meeting, throw a conversational bone to the group by referring to a trend or observation. "Did you see the blog on…?"

If you have a few minutes to devote to one person, ask about her work. How did the executive management group respond to a recent project? What were the hot topics at the recent conference they attended? Tilling familiar soil can yield great surprises beneath the surface.

Flex Time

At any event **small talk matters**. However, spending all your time commiserating about kids or discussing favorite restaurants won't help you show excellence. Using your time budget wisely may require flexing your agenda. We encourage you to set those agenda points free if you notice someone connecting with you on a different topic or glancing away because they're distracted or their interest is waning. Clamping the verbal wheel too tightly to stay your conversational course will leave your audience reaching for the door handle.

A Wabi-Sabi Conversational Win-Win

When Lance, a television programmer, threw his agenda out the window to make way for a better connection, he scored big.

During a round of media training where we encouraged the practice of connection over messaging, Lance almost blew a gasket. No way could he try asking a question of his arch nemesis, the television critic from hell, who continually panned his fall lineup. No matter what Lance said, the guy reacted with a querulous response.

When we asked Lance to describe his own reaction in the face of so much uncalled-for negativity, Lance said he tried to move more quickly through his speaking points. We kindly didn't ask Dr. Phil's standard question: "How's that working for you?" Instead we asked Lance to consider what would happen if he addressed the negativity with a gently probing question. Specifically, we suggested, "I hear from your voice this isn't what you expected, can you tell me why?" We cautioned against calling the critic on his negative tone.

Several days later, we received an excited call from Lance. The results he reported from his interview astonished even us. As usual the critic vented. Tired of the tirade, Lance floated our question and received a surprising confession. The critic had undergone a series of painful foot surgeries that left him little time to review the show tapes Lance sent. In a weird coincidental twist, Lance had experienced a similar surgery and offered up his best pain relief system. The tone shifted, and the critic offered to watch the tapes again. This time the reviews rocked, and Lance learned about the value of connection.

When you're prepared and flexible, your conversations can become explorations. The most important thing to remember about *Wabi-Sabi at Work* communication is that **every exchange is an opportunity for another exchange**. Each conversation—whether in writing or in person—provides a sampling of who you are and should leave your audience wanting more because they enjoyed the exchange.

Aha! to Action: Kick it Up a Notch

Acclaimed chef Emeril Lagasse likes to spice up his dishes. In this Aha! to Action, we borrow from his recipes to take our communications to the next level.

Aha!

Write down three places your communications fell flatter than an undercooked soufflé. Who slammed the door? Was it you, the other person, or the circumstance?

	Person	Place	A Conversational Thud
1.			
2.			
3.			

Action

Identify what you would add or change to make each communication pop.

Possibilities include:

- ✓ A more flexible agenda.
- ✓ An open-ended question.
- ✓ An organized and descriptive anecdote.
- ✓ Active words.
- ✓ A relational touch.

Communication pop # 1:

Communication pop #2:

Communication pop #3:

Wabi-Sabi Grace Notes

✓ *Smooth conversations with no mistakes make people feel like they're just a placeholder in your script; real conversations can be rough around the edges.*

✓ *One brief but interesting story, with an emotional connection, will engage someone more than a laundry list of impressive accomplishments.*

✓ *Asking, as well as sharing information, opens a verbal door and invites someone to step through.*

✓ *Clear away verbal distractions—ambiguous words, fillers and repeats—so others can see you, not your habits.*

Chapter 7
Image Matters

Wouldn't it be great if the people who influence your career recognized you for producing great work, and appearances never entered the picture? We wish this were the case, because many of our clients would have been superstars sooner. A colleague who took casual Fridays too literally learned the hard way how image impacts a career.

While the technology company she joined claimed to be relaxed, in reality only the worker-bees wore jeans. When this newly appointed vice president came in on "casual Friday" wearing a comfy pair of holey jeans and a T-shirt, she had no idea her day to organize her office would be the same

Get noticed for the right things.

You don't have to be a fashion maven or a metrosexual to be noticed. Whether it's your office or your wardrobe, the value you give to what others see and your attention to detail is what sets you apart. You show who you really are by breaking out of uniform ruts and reflecting your personality in your image and surroundings.

day she'd run into the company's elusive CEO. As she entered the elevator and made eye contact, she was appalled to notice his pressed khakis and collared shirt. Before she could open her mouth or extend her hand, the CEO gave her the once-over and turned to talk to someone else. She knew she'd been pegged as an intern. From that day forward, she separated clothes into casual and "too casual" categories. Now on dress-down days, she wears tailored black jeans paired with a crisp, collared shirt, reflecting a sophisticated senior player who is relaxed, but ready to jump into action.

Unfortunately, not everyone experiences such a quick image "aha" they then act upon. We've seen countless professionals tripped up, and held back, because of image, including these stand-outs.

The Baby Blahs

A new mom at a healthcare organization flies into meetings unkempt and bedraggled. When co-workers point out the baby muck on her clothes (a regular accessory), her temper flares. Feeling her right to motherhood is under attack, she acts like the spit-up is a badge of honor instead of a mistake.

There are lots of ways to embrace your role as a new mother without wearing the evidence. A few pictures on the desk say more than muck on a blouse.

Just Rolled Out of Bed

Young and unknowing, our freshman hire didn't see the point of ironing his shirts or polishing his shoes. He also missed that he was the only team member who never met with clients in spite of kudos on his work.

A few minutes of press and shine and he'd have been asked to showcase his talent.

Office Pile-up

A highly creative entrepreneur invites a new client to stop by and talk about an upcoming project. The client's eyes widen with shock when he must pick his way through a landmine of paper stacks.

A few minutes of straightening and organization sets the right tone for productive meetings.

Car Craze

A colleague accepts a ride with a co-worker. As she takes a seat, a hairbrush pokes her in the backside and a leaning tower of CDs spill to the floor. Afraid for her shoes, she gently kicks the old French fries and milkshake cup out of the way.

How you treat your ride says a lot about your personal habits. A quick stop at the Gas N' Go transforms a dumping ground into a haven for off-site conversation.

By now we imagine you're mentally scanning all the places where you show up. Before you hit the panic button, we offer this good news. Polishing your image doesn't take lots of money. Like the Wabi-Sabi tea ceremony, it's not the expense of the utensils and newness of the linens that define a tea master. It's the arrangement and attention to detail—such as setting up a simple vase with one flower to greet visitors—that gives value.

But didn't we say Wabi-Sabi is about embracing imperfection? That's true. The teacup can be chipped and still be attractive. There's a distinct difference between worn and sloppy. By applying the principles of Wabi-Sabi design like simplicity, uniqueness, and appreciating both new and old, there are fresh ways to see yourself and your workspace.

Expressing your *Wabi-Sabi at Work* self visually means giving attention to the details of your appearance and what's around you in an authentic way. It doesn't take a slick image consultant or a high-priced interior designer. All you need is a fresh eye and a mirror. The first step is to eliminate visual distractions and then find a natural extension of your best self based on what attracts your eye, or holds a personal connection.

Discovery Exercise: Wipe Out Distractions

Assess the areas of your professional life where the visual cues you send speak louder than words.

In meetings

How do you enter the room?

Professionals who walk in with a Tasmanian Devil approach are often dubbed disorganized or unprepared long before they say a word.

What kind of handshake do you have? A fracturing squeeze, dead fish, or the royal three-fingered grip?

What's on your table? A mega-mug, stacks of folders, or a buzzing iPhone?
None of these are inherently bad, but if they add to the clutter or distraction around you, it may be worth paring down.

Tips:
- ✓ Take a deep breath, smooth your hair, and straighten those files instead of rushing into a room.
- ✓ Harness excitement or nervous energy at the table by directing it into a useful action.
- ✓ Power up your limp handshake with a firmer grasp. (Go ahead—ask a friend.)

In your work space
Everyone has his or her level of organization, but if there's ever a place where clutter will distract, this is it.

What greets the eye when you first walk in? Is this what you want others to notice about you first and foremost?
A professional with a romantic streak completely covered her cubicle with Valentine decorations. As an executive walked by after hours, he wondered aloud to a visitor (us) whether it was possible to get any work done on the Love Boat.

What personal touches—photos of you partying at a conference, tradeshow swag, or your stress ball—draw the eye?

In your closet…

This area is in your personal domain but will provide you with some important clues about how you approach your image.

What is the overall look and feel of your closet? Would you be proud to show off this area or would you be making a lot of excuses?

What themes do you note? Are you prone to wearing one color, or is a lot of real-estate taken up by accessories?

Spend this week neatening, pressing, and throwing out any item of clothing or object taking up precious space that doesn't showcase your *Wabi-Sabi at Work* strengths or a critical area of your life (travel, important connections, parenthood). With a clean palette to work from, you're ready to start exploring new ways to stand out through image and break out of any ruts you've fallen into.

An Enigma to Herself

Sabina hated to shop, and only ordered her clothes online. The net effect was a bland, standardized uniform of five alternating slacks, skirts and tops in subdued hues that she barely thought about as she dressed each morning. While ease-of-routine drove her fashion sense, Sabina didn't realize the impression she left behind. That all changed the day she ran into a co-worker at the soccer field.

Much to her surprise, the co-worker couldn't stop commenting on Sabina's casual outfit, specifically how much more youthful she appeared.

"At work you dress in such serious clothes—those black suits—I didn't realize you were so current and energized," said the co-worker. Sabrina realized she'd missed an important opportunity to show more about herself to the people at work. She wasn't being sloppy, nor was her clothing inappropriate. Instead, her wardrobe left her looking stuffier and less up-to-date than she felt. She wondered if people thought the same things about her personality and skills.

Sabina represents a whole population of professionals who fall into the uniform rut. Every day they wear A plus B with limited modification. Their appearance says very little about their abilities, enthusiasm, or personality. In following *Wabi-Sabi at Work*, each of us needs to do some shaking up of our image at least a few times in our career. Adding color to your wardrobe or to a space generates a mood. Cool pastels soothe. Yellows and reds energize. Color differentiates you from the sea of beige and black. Whenever we speak at big events, or have a whopper of a client pitch, we wear the colors that make us feel strong and the pieces that inspire our creativity.

Graphic Revelations

Part of being able to express yourself through image is to understand what sparks you visually. To know this, look for common colors, objects, design or themes.

A marketing researcher and business associate uses a collage technique to uncover themes about associations people make with different products. After a pizza campaign with a focus on competitive pricing went awry, our friend was hired to find out why. Her idea? Give people lots of magazines and have them rip out images that screamed pizza. When she gathered all the pictures from her focus groups across the country and tacked them to the wall, one image surfaced over and over again. The sofa. Her interpretation? People relate pizza to informal gatherings. Where? You guessed it. Hanging out on the sofa. The price of the pizza wasn't as important.

What worked for a focus group can work for you. Hang out at the magazine rack and flip through whatever grabs your eye. Check out a local art gallery or antique store. Walk along any city street and think about which buildings attract your attention. Take note of what you pick up, rip out, or spend time examining.

When themes crop up, you may be on the verge of discovering a clue to your *Wabi-Sabi at Work* style. Are you attracted to the modern, clean-lined, and chrome? Or, do you like things comfy and broken in? Do you appreciate open and simple surroundings, or collections of one item, like the client who loved old radios? How does what you love relate to how you do your work and your *Wabi-Sabi at Work* strengths? Casual people often value informal surroundings. The buttoned-down, tech-toy aficionado may gravitate toward the more modern and geometric.

Discovery Exercise: Dream a Little Dream

Maybe you can't afford the office toys of a Google founder or a studio space like the Guggenheim, but you can be inspired by them. Think about your ideal office space. Dream a little with no limitations on budget, size, or innovation.

Describe your fantasy work space.
Windows, entertainment system, iPod, books/magazines, comfy couch, leather executive chair, lamps.

What are the common themes of your style?
Structured/modern, lots of texture and rich colors, open, homey, high-tech, low maintenance.

Now, contrast your fantasy workspace with your reality. How do they compare?

Which elements can you incorporate into your day-to-day life and environments that say something significant about you to others?

Remember Sabina? When she looked at her dream office space, a new person was revealed; one who valued warm tones, comfortable pieces, and ergonomically-designed accessories. She came up with some natural ways of extending her preferences into her professional image and space, including:

- *Visiting boutiques and European design shops (instead of the mall) with her teen daughter who added a more current, youthful perspective.*
- *Integrating confidence-boosting purple into her wardrobe as a signature hue.*
- *Purchasing a small sculpture and print for her office from a local art school.*

It doesn't matter where you find or borrow inspiration. The point is to be inspired while being yourself. Each of us has something we can do with our visual image to better stimulate our passions or highlight our strengths. Use everything you have at your visual disposal to get noticed the way that you want.

Aha! to Action: A Trip to Inspiration Point

Live with anything long enough and it's easy to stop seeing it. You don't have to go far to find inspiration and renew pleasure in your surroundings.

Aha!

Find an object that embodies your personal flare or is significant to you—a special shell found on a beach adventure, a bookend passed on from your grandfather, a small vase, an artistic black-and-white landscape photo, or a piece from nature.

Action

Create an inspirational treasure-spot by placing your object in this location. If you wish, periodically move new and different items into the space.

Wabi-Sabi Grace Notes

✓ *Just like your home expresses your personality, your car and what you wear offer windows into your* Wabi-Sabi at Work *self.*

✓ *The "uniform" you wear to work can hide or differentiate you.*

✓ *An integrated image "shows up" in every aspect of your work, life, and play—the how is up to you.*

✓ *What you spend on your image doesn't count; attention to detail and how you demonstrate value weighs in more.*

Chapter 8
Flip It, Turn It, Redirect It

Somewhere, sometime in your career, you've more than likely fallen on your face. Whether it was a mistake of your own making or a situation that spiraled out of control, treating failure as a "when" not an "if" is the essence of accepting imperfection. At the core of this acceptance is the idea that an imperfection in one setting can be redirected and turned into strength in another. *Wabi-Sabi at Work* allows professional mistakes and career falls to become opportunities drawing on your authentic and natural strengths.

Transform failure and imperfection into career defining strengths.

How do you pick yourself back up after a failure or mistake? Think of the Aikido student who trains for a fall and plans to be back on her feet in a matter of seconds. Wabi-Sabi at Work *is about adapting quickly and using your strengths to stabilize the situation.*

Aikido students train how to fall and step back up in a fluid motion. Flexibility, strategy and quick thinking move the fighter back into a competitive stance. Read the backgrounds on many a CEO and you'll find that headline-makers like Jack Welch and Steve Jobs have fallen, gotten back up, and made more happen as a result of their failures. In this chapter, we'll ensure that you are using your signature strengths as a basis for success and flip, turn, or redirect the situations where "failure" would flatten you.

Leaky Boat, Sink or Swim

Lana, a publicist for a big-name tech company, turned a firing offense into a media coup. During a carefully timed product launch that had taken months to set up, she inadvertently told a local reporter he could print the story early. (He'd cleverly slipped in the question, while she was distracted with a demonstration malfunction.) When she realized what she'd done and asked the reporter to wait, he said, "no." Knowing how most reporters hate to be scooped, Lana worried that the story would be viewed as old news and the coverage would be limited.

However, instead of going down with the leaky ship, Lana kept it real, going for the relationship over the story and working the phones late into the night until she'd reached every single reporter. When they realized the story was big enough to warrant a leak, the same reporters who'd been blasé before paid greater attention. The national coverage proved even better than Lana had hoped.

Unlike Lana, we can't always control a situation and may have less time to respond the way we want. However, being able to read what's happening and draw upon your *Wabi-Sabi at Work* strengths will help you bounce back more quickly and respond authentically with integrity.

The Investigator

Facing a potential career-ending situation, Quinn brought his straight-shooting, analytical strengths into play and without planning to propelled his career forward.

When a new inventory tracking system Quinn had recommended unexpectedly reduced bonuses, senior managers wanted his head. Instead of accepting the scapegoat role and planning his exit, Quinn formed an investigative team. Two weeks and many long nights later, they discovered a discrepancy in inventory numbers related not to Quinn's new process, but to the outdated inventory tracking system. Armed with data and a strong case, Quinn convinced the general manager to retain the new system and address the managers. Ultimately, Quinn's analytic approach resulted in a bonus adjustment.

The win for Quinn included more than exoneration. By stepping forward when he felt like stepping back, he made strong interdepartmental connections and gained support for later operational recommendations. He also earned the GM's respect for his leadership under pressure. At his year-end performance evaluation, his supervisor listed the event as a career success.

Embracing Imperfection

As with Lana and Quinn, in the world of *Wabi-Sabi at Work*, imperfection creates opportunity by revealing underlying character and allowing signature strengths to shine. Lana's relational ability and sense of fair-play helped her flip a bad moment into a major win. Quinn's analytic abilities allowed him to evaluate what was really going on.

These professionals decided to move forward during an imperfect moment. For many people, fear of mistakes really stems from how they will react when the mistake occurs. By being reactive, you shut down the opportunity to make a strong next move. The best way to avoid a knee-jerk response is to identify your typical reaction pattern.

Discovery Exercise: Your Barometric Reading

Savvy professionals weather unexpected storms (or mistakes) by tuning into the atmospheric pressure and then responding. The unprepared react. When you are unsure, what is your duck-and-cover reaction?

✓ A Godfather Moment: Wipes off all fingerprints to remove the evidence; deletes an emotional email or dumps an incriminating file.

✓ Go Ahead, Make My Day: Eager for challenge; confronts a rumor-monger in the hallway, or brings up the situation unexpectedly in a staff meeting.

✓ Scarlet O'Hara: Promises to think about it tomorrow; uses caller ID to avoid answering the phone; flags the emails but never responds.

✓ King of Denial: Adopts the "I did not inhale" attitude; when confronted by a colleague, responds with, "I never said that."

✓ The Apologizer: Hands over the rope to string themselves up; points out the errors in a report before anyone else can.

✓ Group Hugger: Seeks out others for consolation and solidarity; travels from office-to-office discussing the mistake with anyone who many have a sympathetic ear.

If you see yourself among this cast of characters, congratulations! The first step toward replacing quick reactions with strategic responses is recognizing them. You've taken a big step toward weathering a professional lightning hit without melting down.

Weather Patterns

To replace a reaction with an appropriate response, you should understand the type of mistake you're experiencing and why it may be happening (and we hope not over and over again in an insanity-producing way). Whether it's an isolated incident, repeated small blunders, or a character "flaw," you can change course and alter your response forecast. A quick glance at the chart below helps you classify the mistake, identify potential underlying causes, and take a countermeasure.

Type of Mistake	Factors to Address	Survival Skills
An Isolated Incident	Was it in your control? Did you act authentically?	Get in and get out, remain focused on solutions.
Repeated Smaller Mistakes	Link to underlying issues like "I don't care enough," not enough is at stake, this job doesn't bring out the best in me, or too many competing priorities (kids, ailing parent, crisis at hand) make it difficult to manage.	If your job doesn't spark excellence, it's time to find an environmental change. If conflicting priorities are plaguing you, the onus is on you to break the cycle.
Character "Flaw"	Your greatest strength can also be your greatest weakness. When you are called out for a trait, don't dump it.	Evaluate if, when, where, and how you demonstrated your strength and what was the actual tipping point.

One time incidents are the hardest to anticipate and control. That's the type of professional mistake where you spill water on a client or miss an important detail that snowballs into career-killing proportions. A reaction might be to point fingers or analyze the situation to death. Remaining solutions-focused is the best response to keeping your head high and your integrity intact.

Repeated small mistakes, like those pesky typos that aggravate your boss, chronic lateness, or your habit of talking over someone during a meeting, can signal a bigger underlying concern. Typos may mean you're not attentive to detail because you're better at soothing a customer's ruffled feathers. Chronic lateness often stems from being over-scheduled or the desire to achieve as much as possible in the shortest time allotted without leaving room for the unexpected. Speaking over someone may result from your lack of respect or too much enthusiasm. In fact when you add these up, they are all reactions instead of responses. Pay attention to the root cause, and you can make the appropriate change or eliminate the mistakes from happening all together. However, unless you make a change, you risk gaining an unwanted reputation as someone who doesn't care about his job.

Any characteristic, whether being seen as too friendly or too focused, can be perceived negatively given the wrong environment, intensity, timing, or audience. When a talent is highlighted in the wrong place or at the wrong time, it's the equivalent of speaking loudly over a movie soundtrack that ends abruptly. You find you're shouting into a dead silence. What works one moment, may not always work the next.

Dog with a Bone

During an annual review, the supervising manager proclaimed that Miles was too inflexible, like a "dog with a bone." When Miles asked for an example, his manager recounted a brainstorm session in which Miles stuck to one idea he thought was best despite the group's interest in exploring other options.

"But what about when I won't take no for an answer negotiating a vendor price?" asked Miles.

Miles asks a good question. Intractability during a brainstorm makes him an irritant. Substitute the brainstorm environment for a budget conversation and his ability to stick to his guns becomes an asset to the organization.

When negative feedback is given about a trait, the first reaction is for the receiver to put cement shoes on the characteristic and get rid of any evidence that it ever existed. Instead of killing a natural trait, Miles should learn in which settings to turn his ability on full-force and when to flip, turn, or redirect his determination.

The Name Game

The thesaurus has dozens of synonyms for the word direct—straight, unswerving, undeviating, straightforward, candid, open, plain-spoken, upfront, and exact. Think of a prominent leader and those words sound promising.

Now remember any uncomfortable feedback you received about a trait you demonstrated— you were too focused, direct, solutions-oriented, or fill in your own blank. The trait can be as benign as a sibling claiming you're always _____, or a supervisor who asks you to work on being so _____. Now, flip the trait and rename it in as many positive ways as you can. If you were called aggressive, try driven, focused, or tenacious.

No Soup for You!

Remember "The Soup Nazi" episode from *Seinfeld*, the TV series? In it, a cafeteria server moves the line along by dishing out a side of abuse with each serving of soup. While his intensity intimidates, he attracts hordes of curious customers. Like an accident about to happen, they can't look away.

At first glance the soup server's actions appear seriously flawed. However, when you uncover the intention behind the intensity, you find value. The server's intention of speeding the line benefits harried business people snatching a quick lunch. It's the intensity of his action that obscures a potential strength.

In business, you can observe plenty of people who have taken notes from this episode. They regularly bring the wrong level of intensity to a situation. Witness Ed, a shop owner, who sells and repairs lamps. He turned his intensity on an unsuspecting customer who mildly accused him of not acknowledging her presence. As Ed harangued her for being one of those impatient women who expected to be waited on hand and foot, she fled for the door. The sad news here is that Ed's objective—to wait on each person in turn, and give them his full attention—was an asset. However, Ed's intensity and poor word-choice (mixed with some misdirected anger) lost him a customer.

You can learn from Miles and Ed how timing and intensity weaken strengths, like Kryptonite, but it's even better to observe your own past.

Discovery Exercise: 20/20 Hindsight

If hindsight is 20/20, then this exercise is a wonderful tool to help you look back in time and rewrite history.

Name a time when you were called out for a trait or characteristic in an unflattering way.

What was the underlying strength? (Even if it seemed hidden from everyone else?)

How could you have adjusted the timing, intensity, or environment in which the trait was used, so it would have been considered more of strength than a liability?

Examples:

1. The misfire: I told a co-worker who made a big faux pas that she'd screwed up.

My intention was to give an honest assessment and share my insight when no one else would.

My timing was off because: she already felt terrible and I was too direct, which made her feel worse; in fact I made her cry.

What I could have done: been more sympathetic first and offered her the choice of hearing my insight.

2.   The misfire: I overwhelmed a client with ideas on how she could beef up her resume, and she became frustrated.

My intensity was off because I flooded her with too much information, too fast.

What I could have done: asked how I could best help her and then shared a few ideas, leaving the door open for more later.

Now apply these history lessons to your future. What are your tendencies and where are you likely to experience a professional bungle? What can you do if that moment comes up?

Thinking you can "quit whenever you want" is like trying to stop smoking without a nicotine patch. If collaboration is your greatest strength, staying chained to your desk all day—the equivalent of going "cold turkey"—will result in your spending excess time reaching out to people on email or wandering the halls on minor errands. It's better to value what you have than try to change who you are.

The Long Haul

Hang out long enough in a career, and you'll run through cycles of being in the right place at the wrong time, right place at the right time, and wrong place at the wrong time. Mistakes and failure are inevitable. Applying *Wabi-Sabi at Work* allows you to embrace the imperfection and change your perspective from being reactive to proactive. Being ready, adapting quickly, and using your powers for good whenever possible will give you more wins than losses over time.

Aha! to Action: A Quick Recovery

Slipping on a banana peel may happen primarily in cartoons, but in your mind the potential for that kind of blunder may loom like a reality.

Aha!

Think of a challenging situation where you fear making a mistake. Ask yourself, what's the worst that can happen?

Action

If you do something minor, like trip at a podium, owning up to the blunder with a light jest like, "I knew I should have taken those ballet lessons," can help you move forward. A bigger blunder deserves a proportionate response.

Imagine the dreaded event just happened. Now what? Plan your next response.

Wabi-Sabi Grace Notes

✓ *In every career, mistakes or imperfections will happen; how you address them reveals your* Wabi-Sabi at Work *strength.*

✓ *A strength demonstrated at the wrong place, time, or intensity may be incorrectly labeled a flaw.*

✓ *Repeated mistakes generally show a systemic flaw caused by an underlying circumstance.*

Chapter 9
Polar Bear or Monkey

Just because the money and compensation rock doesn't mean you'll survive in a company. Different people, like different species, need the right environment to thrive. Just as monkeys need to climb and polar bears need to swim, you're more likely to do well in an environment where the norms correspond with the way you like to interact and where a company values the types of strengths and talents that you bring along.

Discover a natural work habitat where you can thrive.

Identifying the environments where your Wabi-Sabi at Work self will flourish best takes dedicated effort and an ability to read beyond the website. Even if you need to stay put for a while, have some strategies on hand to keep you primed and ready for opportunity.

Without the right environment, you could eventually lose motivation and stall your career.

Waiting for the perfect place to show up is unlikely. After all, the workplace, like nature and Wabi-Sabi, is imperfect and impermanent. Even in a wonderful environment, imperfection can creep in, via a grouchy co-worker or a system failure. A boom in business or a contraction follows if not a natural cycle, then at least one that changes. As a result, what fits you at one point in time may not at another. Understanding where and under which conditions you will flourish will either aid your career evolution or leave you like a fish out of water.

In this chapter we investigate places and settings. If this sounds a lot like exploring corporate culture, you're partially right. We've found there's more to the culture than how often people hang out together, the energy, or the atmosphere. There are clues like how they like to work, when and under what circumstances—the battlefield or a focused mission—camaraderie emerges. That's why it's incumbent upon you to find your natural fit. One step toward discovery is to explore your roots and the passions and places that fueled your growth before you had to be someone.

Discovery Exercise: When I Grow Up

Asked what they want to be when they grow up and most little kids answer without hesitation. They can already feel the excitement of dancing on point, sliding down a fire pole, or healing the sick.

Ask your inner child what he/she wished to be way back when. What did you spend time dreaming about, or on what activity could you blow a whole day? Write these down.

What do these activities share? Were they happening in exciting, challenging places? Quiet and contemplative spots? Were you helping someone else?

When Elaine remembered her childhood dream of a nursing career (derailed by an aversion to needles), she experienced a serious "aha" moment. She'd transferred her desire to help people into a series of seemingly unrelated jobs ranging from executive assistant to a church pastor to preschool teacher for children with teenage mothers to human resources benefits specialist.

In her worst, shortest-lived job as a customer service rep for a moving company, her helping hands had been tied, and she'd been her most miserable. She'd taken the job for the salary and a better commute without realizing that customer service and assistance were the last things she'd be providing. The entire office culture revolved around quick sales and limited quality assurance. Elaine became the front line for justified customer complaints that she was powerless to resolve. Something had to give—and Elaine decided it was her. She quit and landed a fulfilling role facilitating emergency family leave and injury prevention benefits.

Elaine learned a lesson about environment versus job description. Had she asked questions about how, not what, or noticed tension written all over the employees during her interviews, she may have steered clear of the moving company.

The leap between your past and the environments in which you flourish may not be immediate. Another way Elaine could have explored the environment was to examine who was on top and what they valued most.

Taking It from the Top

Large companies hire a CEO for expertise needed at a specific point in time, and their values and influence generally trickle down throughout the organization. Hewlett-Packard brought on Mark

Hurd, described in business articles as an efficiency expert who could streamline operations and improve financial performance. During Hurd's early days, employees could anticipate a tightening of the purse strings for marketing, advertising, training, or any other expansive or non-essential initiative that didn't yield immediate return-on-investment.

A CEO or company owner's background, personality, and places they've made their career mark can inform you on what will be valued most and the types of efforts that will be most readily rewarded. If a leader builds her name on creating an international brand, expect marketing to rule. A risk taker who has gambled big on an idea and won may create an environment where fresh-thinking (backed by data) is the ticket to visibility.

However, your research into a company's environment doesn't begin and end at the top tier. There are a lot more factors to look into and assess. Some of them are readily available through web-surfing or scanning industry blogs.

A Great Read

Websites embody a company's culture (at least how they wish it would be) through design and copy. Online press room and news sections offer insights into what the organization finds important. If there's a glut of hiring announcements, you should anticipate organizational changes and a general air of uncertainty. This could also spell opportunity to form a new team and get in on the ground floor. Lots of partnerships? The company may be in expansion mode or relying on outside growth. There will be spending, followed by accounting. If you have an aversion for either, you may find you're way outside your comfort zone. This may not necessarily be a deal breaker if other environmental needs are being met.

How a company describes itself—the tone, language, word choices—speaks volumes about the environment. Is it formal or loose? Descriptive or bland? Compare these job section listings from two well-known animation studio websites and glean what each says about the work environment.

Example #1: Studio describing the working environment

Crossing over from one discipline to another is not uncommon—modelers becoming animators and so on. There are even classes to teach folks what they wouldn't normally learn in their regular daily routine. With the amount of time we spend together, a lot of us are as close as family. We have yoga classes, and you'll find us hanging out together on a Friday night at the bowling alley.

Environment potential: collaborative, informal, friendly, holistic, emphasis on cross-training and skill development.

Example #2: Studio how-to for making a demo reel

Just like a resume is no more than two pages unless you've been CEO or a senator, if you have a lot of great material ... do a four-minute version, and then refer to longer pieces on a DVD afterwards if you get that far into the process. For the entire short see the additional materials section ... blah blah blah yackity schmackity.

Translation: light-hearted humor, an air of irreverence, creative solutions, exploration versus standard operating procedure, competitive.

Can't find any updated information about a company? That may be a tell-tale sign of a company that's cash-strapped, doesn't value a public presence, or is in a crunch mode. Whatever you do or don't uncover, surfing the web and reading articles aren't substitutions for being up close and personal.

The Native Habitat

Like a good animal tracker spotting broken branches to tell if there's been conflict or quiet passage, you'll want to move closer to read the signs. Remember, Elaine's great awakening happened after she realized she had missed critical clues about what was going on in her environment.

Discovery Exercise: Spot the Signs

Try your skill at discovering the hidden landscape of a company that's caught your interest.

<u>Climb to the mountain-top</u>: View the company from a 10,000-foot perspective.
Drive by the parking lot at random hours—7 a.m. or 7 p.m. If cars fill the lot well after hours, you're in for a long day or they offer flex time. What about at lunch? Unless they have a world-class cafeteria, you could spend a lot of time eating at your desk.

<u>Walk on the wild side:</u> Poke your head inside the den.

During your interview make the most of being inside. Is the office laid out like a cubicle Habitrail or are private offices the norm? Does the hive buzz with conversation or is it quiet as a tomb? Does collaboration versus independence rule? Is the furniture bargain basement or is there a designer chair at every desk to show you how much image counts? Are people smiling or stressed?

<u>Hang at the watering hole:</u> Observe people acting naturally.

Nearby coffee shops, lunch spots, and after hour hang-outs offer great places to observe company wildlife. Take a book or laptop and listen hard. Watch how people show up. Are they taking business calls while ordering a latte? Beefing about the management after hours? Dressed to the nines or wearing track shoes?

At a local diner, Jhonna overheard sales executives spouting off about their management and sharing confidential information. While this could have been an isolated incident, it matched other things she'd observed during her interview, like loud swearing and yelling over cubicle walls. It was not the courteous or respectful place Jhonna preferred. While she might be able to hack it for the experience, the long-term stress of working in those conditions would require adding longer work-outs and meditation to her already crammed schedule.

Wabi-Sabi at Work doesn't force a fit where none exists, and the more you cull through an environment to see the ins and outs, the more successfully you'll find the right match.

Think of the time and effort you put into deciding your "must have" list when shopping for a vehicle or planning a vacation. Remember, there is much more involved in choosing the environmental elements where you can trajectory your career than the size of the cup holder or the average rainfall in January. So why not give the place as much attention?

Should I Stay or Should I Go?

When counseling people on accepting or changing jobs based on environment, we offer up the lyrics to the Rolling Stones's song "Satisfaction".

"You can't always get what you want, but if you try sometimes, you get what you need."

What determines your needs? To find out, make a list of everything you now know about your dream work environment and the places you've enjoyed working in the past (no matter how they seem unrelated to your current job direction). Now divide the list into three columns, "must have," "nice to have," and "no way." If the majority of your must haves are being met, or there's a specific reason you can't change jobs in the short term (financial dependence, necessary experience), consider another outlet for your *Wabi-Sabi at Work* strengths like the following example of a financial group administrator with a creative flair.

Letting the Inner Creative Out

Glen, a detail-oriented, get-the-job-done guy, devoured graphics programs like some people eat chips. Unfortunately, his daily tasks—editing memos and posting schedules—were much more mundane.

One day Glen ventured to apply his graphics knowledge by changing the font on a standard report. Thinking it was just a fluke when the manager asked him to stick with the old Times New Roman font, he introduced bolder colors to a PowerPoint pie chart. He accompanied the change with a note explaining how the colors translated better on the wall and the layout read more easily for people at the back of the room. Once again, he was asked to go back to the old format. After several more futile attempts, Glen knew he was up against an unmovable force. His options were to leave a secure position for a lateral move somewhere he couldn't imagine or find another outlet for his inner creative.

At our suggestion, he offered his services to an association at his company. There, he took on creating flyers and email blasts to encourage membership. The chance to demonstrate his vision among people who embraced his talent recharged his battery. Eventually his work gained recognition, and he received an invitation to join another department responsible for producing presentations.

Whether it's you or your environment that does the changing, in Wabi-Sabi, change is inevitable. When organizational shifts occur or new products are launched, wild success can follow—and you must find your footing. Knowing which strengths are valued and that showing up to a place each day will be a pleasure, not a chore, are critical to your personal satisfaction and successful professional evolution. Whatever your decision, to stay, go, or explore new territory, knowing how and where you want to take the *Wabi-Sabi at Work* journey will ensure your career distinction versus extinction.

Aha! to Action: Save the Environment

A regular maintenance program, like changing a furnace filter every two months, saves energy in the long run.

Aha!

Where is the energy flow at work? Who's gaining recognition and reward? Why?

Action

Where are you expending energy at work in ways that deplete and drain your entire system? What environment would allow you to tap a more natural power source?

Wabi-Sabi Grace Notes

✓　As in nature and Wabi-Sabi, work environments are imperfect and impermanent.

✓　Where you thrive is based more on how people do their work and interact and less on what the job actually entails.

✓　A top-to-bottom and below-the-surface workplace examination reveals critical information about how people interact and what is valued.

Chapter 10
Are We There Yet?

Great careers, like great journeys, take you places you never imagined and open the world to you in new ways. Even if you've been a planner all your life, hitting every milestone you ever set, there comes a time when personal satisfaction may come from beyond where your eye can see. Or, life throws you a curve ball, like illness or a layoff. Or, your career pathway ends, because there's no logical next step and you're forced to find a new direction.

Wabi-Sabi at Work honors the incomplete and impermanent quality of a professional journey. Whether the landscape shifts so slowly you don't notice, or events cause you to stumble, internal or external changes are inevitable. The good news is that if

Take your next career steps at a comfortable stride.

Your career is a journey where paths unfold and new opportunities lie around the next turn. If you explore your surroundings, interests, and passions, your next big thing may very well be right before you.

the journey isn't over, there's always somewhere else to go. Our goal is to help you to travel down the career road as an explorer, open to possibility.

Think about what it means to be an explorer. Explorers take time to engage in the environment and make decisions based on the moment. They follow their instincts and impulses to build new pathways where none existed before. Sometimes, as in the case of Greg Mortenson, the rock-climber who took a wrong turn and wound up dedicating his life to building a school in the village he stumbled into (described in the book, *Three Cups of Tea*), these side treks can prove to be the most life-altering and fulfilling.

In a speech to Stanford University graduates, Steve Jobs recounted how, unsure of his career path and not wanting to waste his parent's hard-earned money, he dropped out of college after six months. However, he stuck around another eighteen months to visit classes that interested him. His college offered incredible calligraphy courses and there he learned about Serif and Sans Serif type-faces. He followed his natural curiosity without any idea how calligraphy would impact his life. Ten years later he would literally change the face of computers by integrating the first beautiful fonts into the Macintosh® computer. Allowing the time and space to explore his interests yielded rewards he never imagined.

You don't have to drop out of school or quit a job to find your passion. How you ease on down the professional road is as much based on who you are as on circumstance. Push yourself too fast or too far, and your engine can overheat. Travel at your own pace, and your comfort level increases, letting you venture into new surroundings.

There's more than one way to take the journey. In Aesop's Fable, *The Tortoise and the Hare*, both animals have the potential to win a race based on two different travel strategies. One speeds through (but loses due to cockiness), while the other makes progress (and wins) at a slow and steady pace. Imagine these two different animals as professionals approaching a project. The "hares" like to sprint through the job, working round the clock to get a job done, followed by a two-week escape. Taken to the extreme, professionals like these can zero in so fully on a project that during their extended work time they may miss out on what else bears exploring. Rest times become critical opportunities for exploration, like cooking lessons in Italy or camping out in the mountains. During their trip, they may decide to take a sabbatical and attend culinary school or retire to the mountains in ten years. The point is that the quieter moments open possibilities for new exploration and pursuits.

The "tortoise" types prefer to stay in a job for years, but balance their time with classes and social engagements. Too much routine and they run the risk of becoming stuck in a career rut. We encourage these professionals to stretch a little, by joining a new organization or volunteering for a project beyond their current scope of responsibility.

One woman we know, who stayed in her telecommunications job for twenty-five years, pursued a love of holistic healing by attending a yearly workshop on the topic. As her career wound down, we recommended she step up the pace on her passion by asking about volunteer possibilities at her next workshop. She eventually found a part-time paid position that she accepted upon her retirement.

Knowing how you'd like to travel through your career can help you adjust your pace, find new opportunities, and gain a sense of adventure. In this discovery exercise, reap insights into how you've been traversing through your career based on how you like to travel.

Discovery Exercise: Walk, Jog, or Run

Perhaps you routinely take walks to work, for pleasure, or to exercise the dog. Or maybe it's been a while since you've explored anywhere on foot. In any case, now's the time to put on those walking shoes and breathe some unfiltered air for twenty minutes. Once you've taken your walk, you'll be ready to answer the questions below.

After Your Jaunt

Welcome back! Parallels often exist between how we engage in the world and at work. Looking back:

Did you plan for the walk with the correct shoes and clothing or impulsively head outdoors? Compare this with how you take on new projects.

How did you move? Did you run, amble, reach a destination, wander off the planned route, or rest on the bench and absorb your surroundings? How does this compare with the way you approach your daily tasks?

Were you interrupted by the phone, an unexpected situation, or the weather? Did you speak with anyone else? Did you view this occurrence as opportunity, or call off the walk?

What caught your eye or ear? Did you explore along the way, or were you thinking the entire time, barely noticing your surroundings? How does this stack up with where you place your focus at work? Do you live in your head all day or stop and smell the ink cartridge?

Did you have a destination in mind or wander until you found someone or something new to explore? Is there any similarity between this and how you find new career opportunities?

On a recent hike, our friend Hal taught us a wonderful lesson on how his approach to a walk in the woods applies to his career. As we stepped on the trail together, Hal, a nature-lover and television producer, picked up the biggest stick he could find. He explained that it was his standard tool for overturning interesting rocks and poking under mossy stumps. While he probed, we stood back (several paces) watching with fascination as he unearthed centipedes, pointed out bird nests and searched for, but thankfully didn't find snakes. Later, we realized that Hal walked through the woods in the same way he found production work. Whether he had his hands full with a project or wanted a new one, he stayed open to what attracted his attention. When something caught his eye, he probed beneath the surface to uncover something new. At work, this equated to meeting with people without knowing if or how the meeting would benefit him and asking questions without an agenda.

When an advertising agency showed him interest, Hal didn't worry about spending time with people so far removed from the documentary filmmaking he loved. Instead he showed up ready to listen and ask questions. To his surprise, the agency's largest client wanted to underwrite a nature show. Had Hal rejected them as not a fit without discovering more, he may never have achieved some of his best work or earned an Emmy. Who knew when he sat down to explore something off his own beaten path it would propel his career forward in an area he loved?

Six Degrees of Professional Separation

Connecting with other people is where the chemistry happens, sparking new ideas about your journey and transforming your career. When these relationships evolve organically, not as part of your intentional networking, the journey becomes more interesting and spontaneous, allowing the adventurer in you to come out and play.

You never really know who's behind the counter or standing next to you until you ask. To start new connections in a fun and relaxed way (as opposed to over-thinking how a connection can become part of your strategic network) on airplanes or while waiting in the latte line, we play a game called "Six Degrees of Professional Separation." Within the first ten minutes of asking someone about themselves, we usually uncover a shared interest or someone we both know in common.

After attending our workshop on creating professional connections, Marta tried the game everywhere she went, including a trip through the Costa Rican rainforest. While standing in line contemplating a zip line ride 400-feet above a leafy canyon, she noticed a pale and trembling tourist behind her. Marta commiserated with her fellow traveler and eventually asked the woman about herself and the family with her. The woman told Marta they lived in Northern California and that her husband worked for a shipping company. Marta knew one other person in shipping, her neighbor in Marietta, Georgia. Despite the odds, Marta mentioned his name. Amazingly, Marta's neighbor worked for the woman's husband.

When Marta returned home she asked her neighbor for more information about her Costa Rican trail-mate and discovered they had even more in common than she had time to uncover, including school choices for their children (they both liked Montessori) and artistic training. A year later when Marta found herself in Northern California on a relocation scouting trip, she felt very comfortable calling the woman and asking for school and neighborhood recommendations.

Linking people you meet with people you know is another way to open career possibilities. When we attended an human resources association dinner meeting, little did we anticipate that the lively young woman we chatted with at our table would become first a client, and then a member of our team seven years later. Our instinct to invite her to an upcoming workshop launched the relationship. We cemented it when we recommended her for an internal position with a major client. The day-to-day contact gave us even more time to know her, and eventually when she was ready to move on, she became a valued member of our team.

When someone or something grabs your interest, it's the right time to act. If you wait until you're in the perfect frame of mind or have your intention clearly defined, it will be too late. The opportunity passes.

The following discovery exercise puts you in the explorer's seat. You'll follow an impulse to meet new people and go to new places based on an interest, whether it's one you've nursed for years, a glimmer of an idea, or something in between.

Discovery Exercise: Chart New Territory

On this journey, you will explore a topic you've been flirting with, but never devoted your full attention to. Before you over-prepare or decide to carry expectation baggage with you, remind yourself that you're going on this adventure as a learner—just to scout around. All you'll really need is an open mind and an open ear.

Plan your trip route:

Pick a subject you love or one that piques your curiosity, like the environment, creative writing, holistic healing, Pilates, or deep-sea diving.

Scout the landscape:

Check the paper, online, an adult learning course catalog, or anywhere else you can find information to explore your interest. Make a date to attend a local lecture, a green building association meeting, class, or wherever people gather around a subject.

Meet the natives:

Pretend you're in a foreign country. Put aside any initial reaction to the people around you as not part of your tribe. Now, pick someone in the room and find out why they're there and what they love about the subject.

Map your findings:

On a clean piece of paper jot down any connections you made, the things you learned (even if you only validated what you already knew), ideas or questions that arose, or challenges you encountered.

Where do you want to go next? Your options, based on this adventure, are to examine a new topic or go further down the path on this one.

What you gain from this type of adventure may not be clear until a year or even ten years from now. Fresh out of college, Stella landed a job as a marketing manager for a major children's toy company. After a couple of years excelling as the person who could set up systems and improve process efficiency, she decided to apply her skills to the non-profit world and enrolled in a two-year social work program. To support herself while in school, she took a position with a small start-up run out of the owner's home. By the time she completed her degree and internship, she realized her calling was building foundations on which companies could grow. She satisfied her desire to help those less fortunate by steering the start-up in a socially responsible direction with pro bono programs and volunteer time.

People told her she'd wasted her time obtaining a degree she'd never use. Yet, Stella found her social work skills transferred easily into dealing with clients. Plus instead of being promoted into management at a non-profit, which would have removed her from fieldwork, she continued to be hands-on as a volunteer. She never regretted following her interests because in the long run, the time she devoted to them paid off in greater personal and professional satisfaction and income.

Great careers last a lifetime but can zigzag along the way. The *Wabi-Sabi at Work* strengths that propel you forward in one place will work for you in other places as long as you're enjoying the ride. *Wabi-Sabi at Work* honors imperfection; what's honest and authentic. It appreciates the impermanent and the inevitability of change. Whether you follow multiple career paths over a thirty-year span or nurture a great passion through an entire lifetime, we encourage you to value who you are today, stay open to what's around you, and know that you can and will change.

You're never stuck, even if you're standing still. Keep your eyes open, and continue tapping into the people, places and passions around you, whether they make sense right now or not. Forge your path, find your joy, be yourself.

A Resource Guide
The Great Wabi-Sabi Awakening

Expanding Wabi-Sabi into your world, beyond your career, happens when you find new people and passions. There you will build community and connections. As we learned from a tea master, Wabi-Sabi and Nike® have a lot in common—there's no right or wrong way, you "just do it" and recognize the moment. Take action and see what shakes out. Pull a group together and plan a monthly event or show up somewhere you've never been before. The good news is this inspiration doesn't require a trip to Machu Picchu.

If you need some prompts on how to start, here are suggestions based on our own Wabi-Sabi awakenings.

Your Wabi-Sabi Community

Beyond your spouse, best friend, family members, and other people in your core support group, are other Wabi-Sabi-ists in the making. Identifying potential friends interested in authentic connections is as easy as:

- Noticing who you're with when the conversation flows
- Realizing a common interest or passion
- Sharing a new perspective different from your own
- Finding inspiration from an unexpected source

Gwen took on Texas Hold 'Em poker with an eclectic group of women. None of them knew how to play and when they decided to learn, they made a set of Wabi-Sabi rules that encouraged imperfection at the table. They would play a few practice hands at the start of each game and even bent a rule or two in the spirit of learning. They mastered the game in a safe, supportive environment aided by Edith's special Italian sandwiches and several bottles of red. Now they can each hold their own at any poker table.

You can try any variation on Gwen's idea or the ones below to jumpstart your Wabi-Sabi experience.

<u>A Kitchen Moment</u>: Too many cooks don't always spoil the pot, sometimes they discover new flavors. Set out to make a complex dish like Paella or Cioppino. Fiddle with a marinara sauce. Invite people to bring ingredients and take an active role. Read the recipe aloud and then set everyone to work without looking back. Go with the inspiration and recommendations as they flow and forget about creating a perfect dish. Go for the perfect experience instead.

<u>A New Pursuit</u>: Take your interest in green building, sustainable energy, wine tasting, Twittering, Reiki, or politics and show up at an event in your town. Whitney attended a Reelscreen Summit conference to learn about reality television production and made a contact that led her further with a show idea.

<u>A Volunteer Opening</u>: A middle school writing coach volunteer experienced first-hand how engaging kids with a topic took more than the standard lesson plan. When the kids were asked to create a biography, they became hopelessly stuck. The coach took them on a library tour, pulling books from shelves and reading the jacket copy for inspiration. The real journey was how exploring the library's shelves reconnected the coach with an old passion - writing children's books.

Be inspired by the richness of your environment and the strengths, passions, interests, and perspectives of those around you.

Additional Wabi-Sabi Reading

These books made our list because the people in them fall into the inadvertent Wabi-Sabi-ist category or the content can help you apply Wabi-Sabi to other areas of your life.

Branson, Richard. *Screw It, Let's Do It: 14 Lessons on Making It to the Top While Having Fun & Staying Green.* New York: Virgin Books, 2006.

Cameron, Julia. *The Artist's Way: A Spiritual Path to Higher Creativity.* New York, Penguin Putnam Inc., 2002.

Gold, Taro. *Living Wabi-Sabi: The True Beauty of Your Life.* New York: Andrews McMeel Publishing, 2004.

Griggs Lawrence, Robin. *The Wabi-Sabi House: The Japanese Art of Imperfect Beauty.* New York: Clarkson Potter, 2004.

Martin, Steve. *Born Standing Up: A Comic's Life.* New York: Simon & Schuster, 2007.

Miller, Karen Maezen. *Momma Zen: Walking the Crooked Path of Motherhood.* New York: Random House, 2007.

Mortenson, Greg and Renlin, David Oliver. *Three Cups of Tea.* New York: Penguin Group (USA) Inc., 2006.

Queen Noor. *Leap of Faith: Memoirs of an Unexpected Life.* New York: Hyperion, 2003.

Young, Jeffrey S. and Simon, William L. *iCon: Steve Jobs, The Greatest Second Act in the History of Business.* New Jersey: Wiley & Sons, Inc., 2006.

Author Biographies

Whitney Greer

Whitney Greer describes her career path as having more twists and turns than San Francisco's famous Lombard Street. Her extensive, multi-faceted career—stemming from Apple's marketing hallways, to a dozen years as CEO of a national training business, to developing a television show relaunching careers—is a true tale of Wabi-Sabi impermanence and reinvention. In each professional challenge she's taken on, she's reached for and relied on staying authentic. She gladly shares her experiences, stories and tools with those willing to explore and be guided by their unique talents and passions.

Whitney has authored numerous print and online articles (www.whitneygreer.com) on *Building Professional Brand, Telling Your Professional Story,* and *Positioning for Success,* as well as spoken to professional associations and organizations across the country. Her entrepreneurial streak led her to found Thumbprint Communications, Inc. a national training and coaching firm providing consulting to Fortune 500 companies. She inspires her clients with her own reinvention story of founding a company and moving across country three times, while balancing the demands of two children and a traveling spouse.

Gwen Woods

What lessons has a tree-hugging vegetarian choosing to live with her in-laws plus three dogs learned about finding career satisfaction? The path is unexpected and imperfect – and that's okay. **Gwen**

Woods, a national business and career consultant, has spent nearly a decade helping others shift perspective on their careers and define their strengths. From leadership conferences with telecom diversity groups to executive mentoring program development and facilitation with national women's associations, Gwen motivates professionals to move beyond trying to be perfect to being fully themselves.

Promoting a more natural way of being in both work and life means she must walk her own walk. Gwen is composing her next written guide *There's an In-Law Living in My House—How to Survive and Thrive in a Multi-Generational Household* (www.wabisabitalktome.com). Gwen takes the concepts of *Are You Wabi-Sabi?* and breaking out of formulas and brings them to life in regular speaking opportunities for professionals in a range of industries from human resources to technology services.

In reviewing her own professional journey, Gwen has learned to appreciate the journey and connections made along the way. Walking hand in hoof with a giant giraffe named Geoffrey as a marketing and inventory manager at Toys R Us exposed Gwen to Toys for Tots campaigns and unveiling a hospital playroom for a needy, rural community. Her passion for nonprofits took her back to the halls of academia to earn a Masters of Social Work degree. Today, Gwen is transplanting her California roots into her beloved community in Chester, New Jersey involving herself in environmental conservation and "green" building.

Made in the USA
San Bernardino, CA
15 May 2013